THE STORIES OF THE PROPHETS FOR KIDS

40 child-friendly stories for the whole family from the majestic quran and islam (Collection - islamic books)

D1620094

Ibrahim Al-Abadi & Islam Way

Original first edition

All rights, in particular exploitation and distribution of texts, tables and graphics, reserved.

Copyright © 2024 by Book Shelter GmbH

ISBN: 978-3-98929-084-6

Imprint:

Book Shelter GmbH
Aufhäuserstraße 64
30457 Hannover
Germany

THIS BOOK IS FOR

FROM

CONTENTS

1

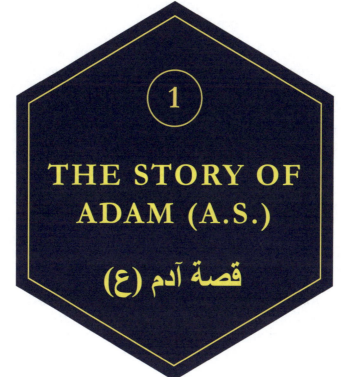

1

THE STORY OF ADAM (A.S.)

قصة آدم (ع)

THE STORY OF ADAM (A.S.)

Hello dear children! This story is about the first people who ever lived. It is found in the Holy Qur'an and is one of the most important stories in Islam.

Once upon a time, a long, long time ago, there was nothing on earth. No people, no animals, no plants - nothing. Everything was dark and empty. But then Allah (s.w.t.) decided to create the world. With His power and wisdom, He began to shape and form the world piece by piece.

First Allah (s.w.t.) created the mountains and hills. Then He formed the valleys and rivers so that the water could flow. It was beautiful to see how the mountains stretched into the sky and the valleys spread out.

Next, Allah (s.w.t.) created the sea. It was wide and deep, with clear blue water. He filled it with many kinds of fish and sea creatures.

After that, Allah (s.w.t.) created the animals of the land. He created majestic lions, swift gazelles, great elephants, and many other wonderful animals. Each had its own beauty and special characteristics.

When Allah (s.w.t.) informed the angels that His next intention was to create human beings as His successors on earth, a certain uneasiness arose among them. They could not understand why Allah (s.w.t.) wanted to create humans, as they had always been the only creatures to fulfill His will.

Some angels expressed concern and asked, "Are You going to create someone on earth who does mischief and sheds blood while we praise You and proclaim Your holiness?" They could not understand how a creature that could be fallible deserved such a place on earth.

Allah (s.w.t.) replied to the angels, "I know many things that you do not know." He revealed to them His knowledge and wisdom beyond all understanding. Allah (s.w.t.) explained that He had given man special abilities that enabled him to live on earth and carry out His commands.

The angels recognized the wisdom and plan of Allah (s.w.t.) and bowed before His will. They accepted that Allah (s.w.t.) would create man as His successor on earth.

Finally, the time had come, Allah (s.w.t.) created the first human being. He formed him from clay and breathed into him the spirit of life. The first man was Adam (a.s.). However, an angel named Iblîs did not accept Allah's (s.w.t.) decision and promised that he would bring disaster upon mankind. Iblîs was then banished by Allah (s.w.t.).

Adam (a.s.) could see, hear, speak, think, and feel, just like us. Allah (s.w.t.) said to him: "I have created you, Adam (a.s.). You are the first human being and I have given you the gift of reason. You will live in paradise and preserve it."

Adam (a.s.) was grateful and felt honored, but he also felt a little lonely. After all, he was the only person in the world and had no company. Allah (s.w.t.), who sees and knows everything, noticed that Adam (a.s.) was lonely. Therefore, He decided to create a companion for Adam (a.s.) to accompany him and keep him company.

From a part of Adam (a.s.), Allah (s.w.t.) created a woman called Hawwa. Like Adam (a.s.), she could see, hear, speak, think, and feel.

Allah (s.w.t.) said to Adam (a.s.) and his wife, "You are the first human beings. You will live together in Paradise and ensure that it is preserved."

They were allowed to do anything and eat anything they wanted. There was only one rule that they had to follow. Allah (s.w.t.) said to them, "There is a certain tree here in paradise. You are allowed to eat any fruit, except the fruit of this tree."

Adam (a.s.) and his wife promised to follow Allah's rule. They lived happily in paradise and enjoyed the beauty and abundance around them, until one day, Iblîs came to them. He was envious of Adam (a.s.) and his wife and wanted to make them break Allah's (s.w.t.) rule. He started a conversation with Adam (a.s.).

"O Adam (a.s.), why don't you eat from this tree? It will bring you wisdom and immortality, and you will be like a god."

Adam (a.s.), who knew of Allah's command, replied, "Allah (s.w.t.) has expressly forbidden us to eat from this tree. He has given us everything we need and warned us of the consequences. We should follow His command and not be deceived by you."

But Iblîs did not give up and turned to Hawwa, "Oh Hawwa, look how beautiful and delicious this fruit is. You will see, it will give you great pleasure to eat it."

Hawwa was torn and began to believe Iblîs' words. She let herself be seduced by her desire and plucked a single fruit from the forbidden tree. She bit into it, then offered it to Adam (a.s.).

Adam (a.s.), who could not hide his love for Hawwa, also allowed himself to be carried away by the temptation; he too took a bite of the forbidden fruit.

They knew immediately that they had made a mistake, feeling shame and regret for what they had done. At that moment, they heard Allah's (s.w.t.) voice calling them, "O Adam (a.s.), have you deviated from what I commanded you? Have you eaten from the tree I told you not to eat from?"

Adam (a.s.) and Hawwa realized their mistake and repented deeply. They asked Allah (s.w.t.) for forgiveness and vowed to remain faithful to Him and obey His commandments in the future. Allah (s.w.t.), the Merciful and Gracious, forgave them, but He also declared that they could no longer remain in Paradise. They had to leave it and live on earth, work, and take care of the world.

They were also to have descendants and teach them to do good and not evil deeds.

And so began the life of humans on Earth. Adam (a.s.) and Hawwa were the first humans, and they had many children. They in turn had children, who had children, and so on, right up to the present day.

The lesson from this story: It is important to follow the instructions of Allah (s.w.t.), even if it is sometimes difficult. Allah (s.w.t.) knows us better than we know ourselves, and He knows what is best for us. If we make a mistake, we should ask Him for forgiveness and try to learn from our mistakes. Just like Adam (a.s.) and Hawwa, we should take responsibility for our actions.

Sources: The Holy Qur'an:

Sura 15, verses 26-39 | Sura 38, verses 71-85 | Sura 2, verses 35-39 | Sura 7, verses 19-27 | Sura 2, verse 37 | Sura 20, verses 115-124 | Sura 3, verses 33-34.

HADITH

قال (صلى الله عليه وسلم-: (إن اللهَ خَلَقَ آدمَ مِن قبضةٍ قَبَضَها مِن جميعِ الأرضِ، فجاءَ بنو آدمَ على قَدْرِ الأرضِ: جاء منهم الأحمرُ، والأبيضُ، والأسودُ، وبينَ ذلكَ، والسَّهْلُ، والحَزْنُ، والخبيثُ، والطيّبُ

He (s.a.w.) said: "Verily, Allah created Adam from a handful taken from all the earths. So, the descendants of Adam came according to the different qualities of the earth: among them, there are red, white, black, and in between. There is also the light, the sorrowful, the evil, and the good."

Narrated by Abu Dawood, authenticated by Al-Albani

DUA

PRAYER FOR FORGIVENESS

رَبَّنَآ ءَامَنَّا فَٱغْفِرْ لَنَا وَٱرْحَمْنَا وَأَنتَ خَيْرُ ٱلرَّٰحِمِينَ

Rabbanā āmannā fa-ġfir lanā wa-rḥamnā wa- anta ḫayru r-rāḥimīna.

Our Lord, we believe; therefore, forgive us and have mercy on us, for you are the best of mercies.

Source: Sura al-MuʿMinun (23:109).

2

THE STORY OF QÂBIL AND HÂBIL

قصة قابيل وهابيل

THE STORY OF QÂBIL AND HÂBIL

A long time ago, when the world was still young, there lived two brothers named Qâbil and Hâbil. They were the sons of Adam (a.s.) and Hawwa, the first human beings created by Allah (s.w.t.) on earth. They grew up together and learned from their parents how-to live in harmony with nature. They also learned that they should do good and refrain from evil.

Hâbil was a shepherd who lovingly looked after his flock. He got up every morning before sunrise to lead his sheep to the lushest pastures. Qâbil, on the other hand, was a farmer who worked in his field, where he grew various types of grain and fruit.

One day Allah (s.w.t.) said to the two brothers, "I want you both to bring me a sacrifice as a sign of your devotion."

Hâbil was excited and said, "I will choose the most beautiful and healthiest sheep from my flock to offer as a sacrifice!" And so, he did. Qâbil, on the other hand, did not think much about it and simply chose some fruits and vegetables. They were not the best he had. When they brought their offerings, Allah (s.w.t.) accepted Hâbil's offering, but not Qâbil's. He became sad and angry. He turned to Hâbil, "Why did Allah (s.w.t.) accept your offering and not mine?"

Hâbil replied gently, "Dear brother, I believe Allah (s.w.t.) has accepted my sacrifice because I gave it wholeheartedly and chose the best I had." But Qâbil was so angry and envious of his brother that in a moment of rage, he attacked Hâbil and killed him. When he realized what he had done, Qâbil felt great remorse and sadness, but it was too late.

Allah (s.w.t.) said to Qâbil, "Your envy and anger have made you do something terrible. You should have been loving and kind to your brother."

Qâbil recognized the value of life and how important it is to treat your fellow human beings with respect and love. Because if someone kills an innocent person, it is as if he has killed the whole of humanity. But if someone saves a life, it is as if they have saved the whole of humanity.

This story teaches us how important it is to be generous and sincere. It also shows us how envy and anger can lead us to do things that we will regret later. We should always try to be loving and kind to our siblings and friends and control our emotions.

> **Sources:** The Holy Qur'an:
>
> Sura 5, verses 27-35.

HADITH

قَالَ رَسُولُ اللَّهِ صَلَّى اللَّهُ عَلَيْهِ وَسَلَّمَ: لا تُقْتَلُ نَفْسٌ ظُلْمًا إِلا كَانَ عَلَى ابْنِ آدَمَ الأَوَّلِ كِفْلٌ مِنْ دَمِهَا، لأَنَّهُ كَانَ أَوَّلَ مَنْ سَنَّ الْقَتْلَ

The Prophet said: "A soul must not be killed unjustly without the son of Adam being partly responsible for it, for he was the first to establish the practice of killing."

Sahih Al-Bukhari 3335,
Sahih Muslim 1677

DUA

PRAYER FOR THE FOR PROTECTION FROM THE DEVIL

رَّبِّ أَعُوذُ بِكَ مِنْ هَمَزَاتِ ٱلشَّيَاطِينِ وَأَعُوذُ بِكَ رَبِّ أَن يَحْضُرُونِ

Rabbi a'ūdhu bika min hamazāti š-šayāṭīni wa-a'ūdhu bika rabbi 'an yaḥḍurūni.

Source: Abu Dawud 4/12

O Allah, I seek refuge in You from the whisperings of the demons, and I seek refuge in You, O Allah, so that they may not be with me.

3

NÛH (A.S.) AND THE GREAT FLOOD

نوح (ع) والطوفان العظيم

NÛH (A.S.) AND THE GREAT FLOOD

Once upon a time, there was a God-fearing man named Nûh (a.s.). He lived during a time when humanity had flourished in numbers but had strayed far from the path of Allah (s.w.t.). They worshipped idols and behaved unjustly towards each other. The rich did not help the poor and thought only of themselves and how they could increase their wealth.

Allah (s.w.t.) saw the injustice and wickedness in the world and decided to do something about it. He chose Nûh (a.s.), a right-eous and good man, to show people the right way. Allah (s.w.t.) said to Nûh (a.s.), "Tell the people to be fair to each other and stop doing evil things. Tell them that they must change. Warn them so that they return to the right path and remind them of the consequences of their evil behavior."

Nûh (a.s.) was a very patient man, so he went to his people and said, "People, we must stop living like this! We must stop worshipping false gods and behaving unjustly. Allah (s.w.t.) has shown us a better way, we should follow it."

But people only laughed at Nûh (a.s.) and did not listen to him. They made fun of him and said, "You are a fool, Nûh (a.s.). Why should we listen to you?" One shouted, "Look at him standing there telling us what to do! As if he is something special!"

Despite the rejection, Nûh (a.s.) did not give up. He continued to preach, day after day, year after year, but the people did not change.

Finally, Allah (s.w.t.) spoke to Nûh (a.s.) again, "They will not listen, Nûh (a.s.). It is time to punish the people. Build an ark, because there will be a great flood that will wipe everything away."

Nûh (a.s.) followed His instructions and began to build the ark. He worked hard, day and night, to complete the ship. People made fun of him and said, "Look at Nûh (a.s.), he is building a ship on dry land. Has he gone mad?"

When the ark was finished, the flood came. It rained for days without a break. The water rose and rose until it covered everything. Before the flood rose dangerously high, Allah (s.w.t.) turned to Nûh (a.s.) again, "Now is the time to gather the animals. Bring one male and one female of each species into the ark."

Nûh (a.s.) and his family entered the ark together with pairs of all kinds of animals that Allah (s.w.t.) had ordered him to save. As the water rose higher and higher, Nûh (a.s.) noticed that one of his sons was not on board the ark. He called out to him, "My son, come quickly! Get into the ark before it is too late!"

His son was stubborn though and shouted back, "No, father, I'd rather climb that mountain over there. I will be safe from the water up there!" Nûh (a.s.) replied anxiously, "There is no protection from the will of Allah (s.w.t.) except He grants it! Please come!"

His son did not listen, and the water continued to rise. Nûh (a.s.) had to watch helplessly as the floods swept his son away. It broke his heart.

Nûh (a.s.), his other family members, and the animals remained in the ark while the flood destroyed the world outside and swept over the wicked people. Even those who had sought shelter in tall trees or mountains perished in the floods.

After the water receded, Nûh (a.s.) spoke to Allah (s.w.t.) and said, "O my Lord, my son was a part of my family. How could this have happened?" He replied, "O Nûh (a.s.), he was not a part of your family because he acted wrongly. You must accept what has happened."

Nûh (a.s.) understood that he had to accept that not all decisions people make are right. He was sad but thanked Allah (s.w.t.) for saving the others from the floods.

Finally, with the water slowly disappearing, the ark landed on a mountain called Al-Jûdi. Allah (s.w.t.) said to Nûh (a.s.), "O Nûh (a.s.), leave the ark in peace and safety! And I will put blessings on you and on the people who are with you."

Nûh (a.s.), his family, and the animals left the ark and thanked Allah (s.w.t.) for their salvation. From that moment on, life on earth began anew.

The lesson from this story is that we should always listen to Allah (s.w.t.) and trust Him, even if the people around us do not and try to dissuade us from believing. We should be patient and persevere even when we are met with rejection and ridicule.

Source: The Holy Qur'an:

Sura 7, verses 59-64 | Sura 11, verses 25-49 | Sura 71, verses 1-28 | Sura 11, verses 36-48 | Sura 23, verses 23-30 | Sura 11, verses 44-48 | Sura 26, verses 105-120.

HADITH

عَنْ أَبِي سَعِيدٍ قَالَ، قَالَ رَسُولُ اللهِ صلى الله عليه وسلم ‹‹يَجِيءُ نُوحٌ وَأُمَّتُهُ فَيَقُولُ اللهُ تَعَالَى هَلْ بَلَّغْتَ فَيَقُولُ نَعَمْ، أَىْ رَبِّ. فَيَقُولُ لِأُمَّتِهِ هَلْ بَلَّغَكُمْ فَيَقُولُونَ لاَ، مَا جَاءَنَا مِنْ نَبِيٍّ. فَيَقُولُ لِنُوحٍ مَنْ يَشْهَدُ لَكَ فَيَقُولُ مُحَمَّدٌ صلى الله عليه وسلم وَأُمَّتُهُ، فَنَشْهَدُ أَنَّهُ قَدْ بَلَّغَ وَهُوَ قَوْلُهُ جَلَّ ذِكْرُهُ {وَكَذَلِكَ جَعَلْنَاكُمْ أُمَّةً وَسَطًا لِتَكُونُوا شُهَدَاءَ عَلَى النَّاسِ} وَالْوَسَطُ الْعَدْلُ

Abû Sa ,îd reported that the Prophet said:
"On the Day of Resurrection, Nûh will come with his people, and Allah will ask him, 'Did you deliver my message?'
Nûh will answer: 'Yes, Lord!
Allah will then ask his community, 'Did he deliver it to you?'
They will say: 'No, no prophet has come to us!
Then he will turn to Nûh and ask him, 'Who can bear witness for you?
He will answer: 'Muhammad and his community!
And this church will testify that he has delivered the message of his Lord to his people.
This is the word of Allah: '{So We have made you a righteous community that you may be witnesses among men}. And 'al-wasat' (the righteous) refers to righteousness."

Sahih Al Bukhari 3339

DUA

PRAYER FOR FORGIVENESS OF SINS (DURING PROSTRATION)

اللهُمَّ اغْفِرْ لِي ذَنْبِي كُلَّهُ دِقَّهُ، وَجِلَّهُ، وَأَوَّلَهُ وَآخِرَهُ وَعَلاَنِيَتَهُ وَسِرَّهُ

Allāhumma gh-fir li dhanbi kullahu diggahu wa-jillahu wa-awwalahu wa-ākhirahu wa'alāniyatahu wa-sirrahu.

O Allah, forgive me all my sins, the small and the great, the old and the future, the obvious and the hidden.

Source: Muslim
1/350

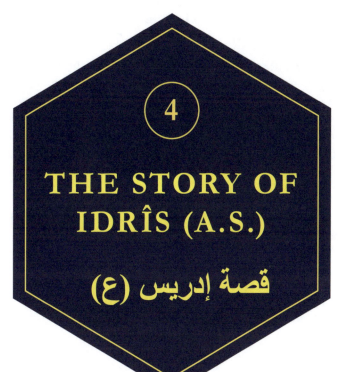

4

THE STORY OF IDRÎS (A.S.)

قصة إدريس (ع)

THE STORY OF IDRÎS (A.S.)

A long time ago there lived a man named Idrîs (a.s.), a great-grandson of Nûh (a.s.). Idrîs (a.s.) was a special person and was known for his great wisdom and his deep faith in Allah (s.w.t.).

Idrîs (a.s.) lived in a time when people gradually began to forget Allah (s.w.t.). They were more concerned with their welfare and pleasure and forgot to honor and worship Him. But not Idrîs (a.s.), he always remained faithful and grateful to Allah (s.w.t.). He showed his loyalty in many ways; like praying daily and leading a life of modesty and simplicity. He always made sure to use his time wisely by praying, meditating, and reflecting on the creation of Allah (s.w.t.).

One day Allah (s.w.t.) spoke to Idrîs (a.s.) and said, "Idrîs (a.s.), you are a good and righteous person. You have always believed in me and worshipped me, even when the people around you did not."

Idrîs (a.s.) was very touched by these words and replied, "O Allah (s.w.t.), I am always faithful to You. Everything I have comes from You. I will always honor and worship You."

Allah (s.w.t.) was pleased with Idrîs (a.s.) and his devotion. As a sign of His appreciation, Allah (s.w.t.) elevated Idrîs (a.s.) to a high rank and gave him special wisdom and knowledge, and Idrîs (a.s.) thought to himself, "I must share this knowledge with all people so that they too can educate themselves!"

So Idrîs (a.s.) began to teach people many useful things. Imagine, people didn't know how to write back then! Can you imagine a life without writing and reading? Without books, letters, and messages? That would be boring, wouldn't it?

So Idrîs (a.s.) thought to himself, "We have to change that!" He took a stick and showed the people how to write letters in the sand. The people were thrilled! But that is not all! Idrîs (a.s.) was also incredibly good at math. He showed the people how to count and calculate. This was extremely helpful and made everyday life and trade easier for many people.

Idrîs (a.s.) also taught people how important it is to be kind and just, and he showed them how to live in harmony with nature and how to resolve conflicts peacefully. He emphasized the importance of honesty and fairness and admonished people never to cheat or treat anyone unfairly.

He said: "We must help each other and take care of each other. And we must not forget to always thank Allah (s.w.t.) because He has given us all these wonderful things!"

Idrîs (a.s.) fortunately was not only a wise teacher, he was also a great prayer leader. He led people in prayer and helped them to strengthen their connection to Allah (s.w.t.). He explained to them the importance of prayer and how it can help them to strengthen their faith and build their character.

However, many people did not use their newfound knowledge of the sciences to do good for others or to strengthen their faith or character. Unfortunately, they sought great wealth and power and used their newly acquired knowledge mainly for this purpose.

The lesson from this story: The story of Idrîs (a.s.) teaches us the importance of education and knowledge. Idrîs (a.s.) used his knowledge to teach and guide people, and we should do the same. We should always strive to learn more and use our knowledge to help others. Just like Idrîs (a.s.), we should always believe in Allah (s.w.t.) and be grateful to Him no matter what.

Sources: The Holy Qur'an. However, it should be noted that the Qur'an does not give many details about the life of Idrîs (a.s.). Therefore, some details of this story come from Islamic traditions and interpretations.

Sura 19, verses 56-57 | Sura 21, verse 85.

HADITH

قال -صلى الله عليه وسلّم-: فَلَمَّا خَلَصْتُ إِلَى إِدْرِيسَ قَالَ هَذَا إِدْرِيسُ فَسَلِّمْ عَلَيْهِ فَسَلَّمْتُ عَلَيْهِ فَرَدَّ ثُمَّ قَالَ مَرْحَبًا بِالْأَخِ الصَّالِحِ وَالنَّبِيِّ الصَّالِحِ

The Prophet Muhammad, may God's blessings and peace be upon him, reported: "When I reached Idris, he said: 'This is Idris, so greet him. So, I conveyed my greeting, and he returned it. Then he said, 'Welcome to the righteous brother and the righteous prophet. "

Sahih al-Bukhari: 3887

DUA

PRAYER BY THE END OF A MEETING

سُبْحَانَكَ اللهُمَّ وَبِحَمْدِكَ، أَشْهَدُ أَن لا إِلَهَ إِلَّا أَنْتَ أَسْتَغْفِرُكَ وَأَتُوبُ إليك

Subhanaka allāhumma wa bihamdika, 'ašhadu 'an lā ilāaha illā 'anta, 'astagfiruka wa 'atubu 'ilayka.

Praise be to You, O Allah and praise be to You. I testify that there is no deity but You. I ask Your forgiveness and I repent to You.

Source: An-Nasa'i, 'Amalul-Yawm wal-Laylah, no. 308

5

THE STORY OF HÛD (A.S.)

قصة هود (ع)

THE STORY OF HÛD (A.S.)

When the descendants of Nûh (a.s.) spread across the earth, they became overconfident, oppressed the weaker ones, and waged wars. The powerful people of 'Ad also lived at that time. They were strong and advanced and built impressive houses in their city of Iram, which was also known as "Iram of the Pillars". Although they had so much, they forgot Allah (s.w.t.), worshipped other gods, and treated the common people unjustly.

Then Allah (s.w.t.) sent the Prophet Hûd (a.s.) to them. Hûd (a.s.) was one of them, a man from the tribe of 'Ad. He went to the leaders and said, "I am here to give you an important message from Allah (s.w.t.). He wants you to stop being selfish and mean. You must start caring for others and be grateful for all the good you have."

One of the leaders laughed and said, "Why should we listen to you? Look at us! We are strong and powerful! What could possibly happen to us?" Hûd (a.s.) looked him firmly in the eye and replied, "Power and wealth are not everything. Why do you worship these false gods? There is only one God, Allah (s.w.t.), whom we should worship. If you do not stop doing bad things and do not learn to be grateful, He will be unhappy and may harm you."

The people of 'Ad laughed and said, "Hûd (a.s.), you are a fool. Our gods have given us all this splendor and strength. Why should we give them up? And who are you to tell us that?" Hûd (a.s.) replied, "Allah (s.w.t.) has given you all these things, not your gods. He made you strong and gave you this city; but you have forgotten to thank Him and worship Him."

Hûd (a.s.) went on to say to the leaders, "Do you remember Nûh (a.s.) and the great flood? That happened because people forgot to be grateful and righteous. The flood was a result of their bad behavior and lack of understanding. Do you want something like this to happen to you? Allah (s.w.t.) will make you disappear from the earth as if you had never existed!"

The leaders only laughed louder at his words.

Then Hûd (a.s.) turned to those who believed him and said, "Come, my friends. It is time for us to leave this city. Let us go to a place where we can live in peace and harmony."

The group followed Hûd (a.s.) and they left the city of Ad' together. They wandered through the desert until they found a peaceful place where they settled down.

Meanwhile, dark clouds gathered over the city of Ad'. A violent storm broke out, stronger than anything the people had ever seen. The wind whipped through the streets and the tall towers that the people had been so proud of began to collapse. The city of Ad' was destroyed and covered by sand, just as Hûd (a.s.) had warned. The idolaters who had not listened to Hûd (a.s.) and mocked him were swept away in the storm.

The lesson from this story is that pride and arrogance can lead us astray from the right path. Even if we are powerful and rich, we must never forget to thank and worship Allah (s.w.t.). For all gifts and blessings come from Him.

Sources: Holy Qur'an:

Sura 7, verses 65-72 | Sura 11, verses 50-60 | Sura 26, verses 123-140 | Sura 46, verses 21-26.

HADITH

قالَ أبو بَكْرٍ رضيَ اللَّهُ عنهُ: يا رسولَ اللَّهِ قد شِبتَ، قالَ: شيَّبتني هودٌ، والواقعةُ، والمرسلاتُ، وعمَّ يتَساءَلُونَ، وإذا الشَّمْسُ كُوِّرَتْ

Abu Bakr said, "O Messenger of Allah, you have grown old." The Prophet replied: "Hud (11), Al-Waqi'a (56), Al-Mursalat (77), Amma Yatasa'aloon (30), and Takweer (81) have aged me."

At-Tirmidhi 3297

DUA

PRAYER FOR FORGIVENESS AFTER COMMITTING A SIN

اللهُمَّ اغْفِرْ لِي مَا قَدَّمْتُ وَمَا أَخَّرْتُ، وَمَا أَسْرَرْتُ وَمَا أَعْلَنْتُ، وَمَا أَنْتَ أَعْلَمُ بِهِ مِنِّي، أَنْتَ الْمُقَدِّمُ وَأَنْتَ الْمُؤَخِّرُ، وَأَنْتَ عَلَى كُلِّ شَيْءٍ قَدِيرٌ

Allahumma, ighfir li ma qad-damtu wa ma akhkhartu, wa ma asrartu wa ma a'alantu, wa ma anta a'lamu bihi minni. Anta al-muqaddim wa anta al-mu'akhkhir, wa anta 'ala kulli shay'in qadeer.

Source: Muslim 1/534

O Allah, forgive me for what I let precede, for what I postponed, for what I concealed, and for what I did blatantly, and for what I was immoderate in against myself, and for what You are more knowledgeable about than I am. You are the Forerunner and the Deferrer; You are the Almighty.

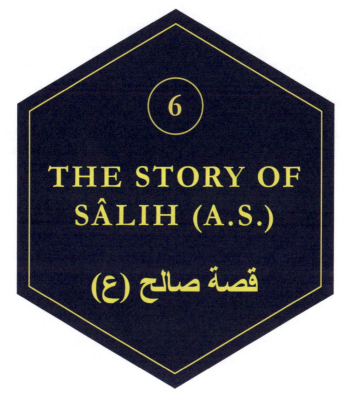

THE STORY OF SÂLIH (A.S.)

قصة صالح (ع)

THE STORY OF SÂLIH (A.S.)

Once, a long time ago, there was a city called Thamûd. It lay deep in the heart of a desert, protected by high cliffs and mountains. The people of Thamûd were very skillful. They built their houses directly into the rock. The city was beautiful and prosperous, but the people of Thamûd were proud and arrogant. The rich took advantage of the poor, demanded high taxes from them, and erected idols that they worshipped.

One day, a young man named Sâlih (a.s.) became a Prophet of Allah (s.w.t.). Sâlih (a.s.) was a good person, always kind and just. He loved Allah (s.w.t.) and wanted the people of Thamûd to do the same.

They said to Sâlih (a.s.), "Look at our city! Look at what we have created with our own hands!"

"Listen, dear children," Sâlih (a.s.) began in a gentle voice, "Allah (s.w.t.) loves us very much and wants only the best for us. We owe all this to Him. Let us thank Him and worship Him."

But the rulers of Thamûd only laughed and said, "Why should we worship Allah (s.w.t.)? We have everything we need. Look at our city! Look at what we have created with our own hands!"

Sâlih (a.s.) shook his head sadly and said, "Yes, you have created much, but who gave you the ability to do so? Who gave you the mountains in which you built your houses? Who gave you life? It was Allah (s.w.t.). Therefore, we should worship Him and thank Him."

The people laughed louder and louder. "Only the destitute and beggars follow you! If you speak the truth, prove it!" they shouted. "Give us a sign that Allah (s.w.t.) exists!"

Sâlih (a.s.) prayed to Allah (s.w.t.) and asked for a sign.

Shortly afterward, he set off into the mountains and returned to Thamûd with a beautiful camel. It was a large, strong camel, the likes of which the people had never seen before.

"This is your sign," said Sâlih (a.s.). "This camel was created by Allah (s.w.t.). It should live freely in the city, and no one should disturb it."

People were amazed at the camel, and some began to believe the words of Sâlih (a.s.); but others were still proud and arrogant. They still did not believe Sâlih and thought him to be a deceitful magician. They refused to acknowledge Allah (s.w.t.) and one day they killed the camel. They wanted to see what would happen next.

When Sâlih (a.s.) heard this, he was sad. "O people of Thamûd," he cried, "why have you done this? You have not respected Allah's (s.w.t.) signs. Now there will be a punishment for you." The rich did not believe him and celebrated their success. They were sure that now the poor would also understand that Sâlih (a.s.) was not a messenger.

Sâlih (a.s.) said to them, "You can continue celebrating in your houses, but remember that you only have three days left. After that, it will be as if these houses never existed!"

The rich people did not heed Sâlih's (a.s.) words and continued to celebrate, but Sâlih (a.s.) and his followers withdrew from the city because they knew that something bad was about to happen.

Suddenly, the ground in Thamûd began to shake because Allah (s.w.t.) sent an earthquake. It was a slight tremor at first, but then it became stronger and stronger. People looked at each other in shock and wondered what was going on. The earth shook and shuddered so violently as if it were scared itself. The beautiful houses they had built in the mountains began to shake. Cracks appeared in the walls and stones fell from the ceilings. The people tried to flee, but the earth shook so much that they could barely walk. A short time later, the city of Thamûd was destroyed.

When the earthquake stopped, nothing was as it once was. The magnificent houses were destroyed, the wells dry, the fields devastated. The people of Thamûd, who had boasted so much about their achievements, were dead. Only Sâlih (a.s.) and those who believed in Allah (s.w.t.) and had fled to safety were spared.

The people of Thamûd had not listened to the warnings of Sâlih (a.s.), and now they had been punished for their disbelief and arrogance. Sâlih (a.s.), who had foreseen all this, was deeply saddened by the fate of his people, but he knew that he had done everything he could to warn them. The people of Thamûd became a warning to all others who disobey Allah's (s.w.t.) commandments.

The lesson of this story: We should always respect Allah's (s.w.t.) signs and obey Him. We must never forget that all our abilities and prosperity come from Allah (s.w.t.).

Sources: Holy Qur'an:

Sura 7, verses 73-79 | Sura 11, verses 61-68 | Sura 26, verses 141-159 | Sura 27, verses 45-53.

HADITH

قال رسول الله صلى الله عليه وسلم وهو بالحجر لا تدخلوا على هؤلاء المعذبين إلا أن تكونوا باكين فإن لم تكونوا باكين فلا تدخلوا عليهم أن يصيبكم مثل ما أصابهم

The Prophet Muhammad said in the Hijr: "Do not visit those afflicted unless you weep. If you do not weep, do not visit them, lest an evil similar to the one that has befallen them befall you."

Sahih al-Bukhari and
Sahih Muslim

DUA

PRAYER FOR MERCY IN DIFFICULT SITUATIONS

اللّهُمَّ رَحْمَتَكَ أرْجُو فَلاَ تَكِلْنِي إِلَى نَفْسِي طَرْفَةَ عَيْنٍ وَأَصْلِحْ لِي شَأْنِي كُلَّهُ لاَ إِلَهَ إِلاَّ أَنْتَ

Allāhumma raḥmataka arjū falā takilnī ilā nafsī ṭarfata `ayn, wa aṣliḥ lī sha‘nī kullahu, lā ilāha illā anta.

O Allah, it is Your mercy that I hope for, and do not leave me to myself for a moment and improve all my affairs; there is no deity except You.

Source:
Sunan Abī
Dāwūd 5090

بِسْمِ اللهِ الرَّحْمَنِ الرَّحِيمِ

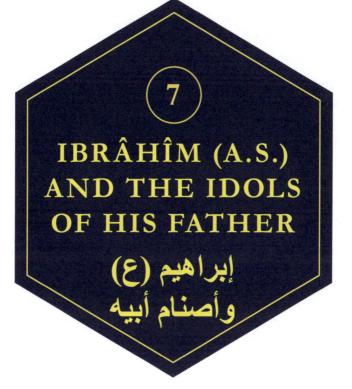

7

IBRÂHÎM (A.S.) AND THE IDOLS OF HIS FATHER

إبراهيم (ع)
وأصنام أبيه

IBRÂHÎM (A.S.) AND THE IDOLS OF HIS FATHER

Ibrâhîm (a.s.) lived a very, very long time ago in a city called Ur, located in modern-day Iraq. People there worshipped many different idols. They worshipped the sun, the moon, and the stars as gods. But Ibrâhîm (a.s.) was different, he believed in only one god - Allah (s.w.t.).

Azar, Ibrâhîm's (a.s.) father, was a respected man who made idols and sold them to people. Every day, Ibrâhîm (a.s.) saw his father carefully shaping the idols and then selling them to the people who worshipped them. But Ibrâhîm (a.s.) could not understand how people could worship something made of wood or stone and created by a human being.

"Father, why do you make these idols? They can neither see nor hear nor help us."

His father replied with pride in his voice, "My son, this is the tradition of our ancestors. People worship the heroes of the past and believe that they bring them good luck." Ibrâhîm (a.s.) shook his head and said, "But father, this makes no sense. These idols are made of wood and stone. They cannot do anything. They don't even eat the food you offer them as sacrifices."

His father became angry and said, "Ibrâhîm (a.s.), these are dangerous words! You should not go against the traditions of our ancestors. People pay me good money for these idols."

One clear night, the young Ibrâhîm (a.s.) went out to watch the sky. He saw the stars twinkling and thought. When he saw a particularly bright star in the sky, he exclaimed, "That could be my Lord!" But after a while, he watched as the star slowly faded in the sky and eventually disappeared. "No, that cannot be my Lord," murmured Ibrâhîm (a.s.), "my Lord would not just disappear."

Later that night, he saw the moon rise, large and bright. He was fascinated and thought that this could be the Lord he was looking for. "That must be my Lord!" he whispered full of hope. Yet as the night passed, he saw the moon grow smaller in the sky and finally disappear. "No, that can't be my Lord either," thought Ibrâhîm (a.s.) sadly. "My Lord would not set." Then when the sun rose the next morning, it was large and radiant. "It must be my Lord; the sun is greater than everything else!" he exclaimed.

But the sun also set in the evening, and Ibrâhîm (a.s.) realized that none of these celestial bodies he had observed could be his master. Then Ibrâhîm (a.s.) said in a firm voice, "I have turned my face to the One who created the heavens and the earth. I follow the true faith and will not serve any idol."

Ibrâhîm (a.s.) understood that there must be a Creator who was more powerful than anything he could see in the sky. He realized that this Creator was Allah (s.w.t.) and decided to serve Him alone and be faithful to Him. He became His Prophet and urged people to turn to Allah (s.w.t.), the only God.

Ibrâhîm (a.s.) said to the idolaters, "Can these idols protect you if they are made of wood and stone? How can they help you when they cannot even help themselves?"

The people were angry but also confused. They did not know what to say. Ibrâhîm (a.s.) had a plan. He wanted to show the people that the idols had no power. So, he waited until everyone was at a festival and no one was near the idols. Then he took an axe and went to the temple where the idols were. He destroyed all the idols and hung the axe around the neck of the largest idol.

When the people returned and saw what had happened, they were shocked and wondered who could have done it. Ibrâhîm (a.s.) said, "Perhaps the greatest idol did it. Look, he is wearing the axe around his neck." But the people replied, "But Ibrâhîm (a.s.), that is nonsense! Idols cannot move!"

Then Ibrâhîm (a.s.) replied, "Then ask yourselves why you worship them. Why do you worship something that cannot speak, hear, or do anything?" The people were speechless because they understood that Ibrâhîm (a.s.) was right. But instead of listening, they became angry with Ibrâhîm (a.s.) because they now realized that he had destroyed their idols. They could hardly believe that one of them, and the son of the man who made the idols, could do such a thing. They feared for their power because if there was only one god, they would no longer be able to intimidate and control the population with their idol stories.

Ibrâhîm's (a.s.) father was also disappointed and angry with his son. He could not understand why his son had destroyed the idols that he had made with so much effort and love. He said to Ibrâhîm (a.s.), "Why have you done this, my son? These idols are our livelihood!"

But Ibrâhîm (a.s.) answered his father lovingly, "Father, these idols cannot do us any good. They can neither speak nor hear and they certainly cannot help us. They are only made of wood and stone. We should only worship Allah (s.w.t.), who has given us everything we have."

Despite Ibrâhîm's (a.s.) explanation, his father could not understand and remained angry with his son. Not only his father but also the other people in the city were angry with him. They decided to punish Ibrâhîm (a.s.) by making a big fire and throwing him into it. They thought that they could avenge their idols by doing so.

Do you know what happened next? Allah (s.w.t.) protected Ibrâhîm (a.s.)! He made the fire cool and safe for Ibrâhîm (a.s.). So, the fire could not harm him. When the people saw Ibrâhîm (a.s.) coming out of the fire the next day rested, they were very astonished. Some of them even began to believe in Allah (s.w.t.).

Nevertheless, Ibrâhîm (a.s.) left his hometown and traveled for many years to follow the words of Allah (s.w.t.) and spread the message of monotheism - the worship of only one God. Before he set off, Ibrâhîm (a.s.) said to his father, "Peace be upon you. I will ask Allah (s.w.t.) to forgive you. Father, I will go and hope that one day you will see the truth."

The lesson from this story: History teaches us that it is important to always seek the truth, even if it may be uncomfortable. Ibrâhîm (a.s.) had the courage to fight against what everyone else was doing because he knew it was wrong.

Sources: Holy Qur'an:

Sura 6, verses 74-83 | Sura 21, verses 51-70 | Sura 26, verses 69-104 | Sura 19, verses 41-50.

HADITH

عَنِ ابْنِ عَبَّاسٍ، قَالَ: كَانَ آخِرَ قَوْلِ إِبْرَاهِيمَ حِينَ أُلْقِيَ فِي النَّارِ: حَسْبِيَ اللَّهُ وَنِعْمَ الْوَكِيلُ

Ibn Abbas reported: "The last words of Ibrahim when he was thrown into the fire were: 'Allah is sufficient for me as a protector, and how excellent He is as a protector!"

Sahih al-Bukhari 4564

DUA

PRAYER FOR FORGIVENESS FOR ONESELF, PARENTS AND THE BELIEVERS

رَبَّنَا ٱغْفِرْ لِي وَلِوَٰلِدَيَّ وَلِلْمُؤْمِنِينَ يَوْمَ يَقُومُ ٱلْحِسَابُ

Rabbanā ġfir lī wa-li-wālidayya wa-li-l-mu'minīna yawma yaqūmu l-ḥisābu.

O Allah, forgive me and my parents and the believers on the Day of Judgment.

Source: Sura Ibrâhîm (14:41)

8

IBRÂHÎM'S
(A.S.) TRAVELS

رحلات ابراهيم (ع)

IBRÂHÎM'S (A.S.) TRAVELS

Ibrâhîm (a.s.) traveled together with his nephew Lût (a.s.) and some followers who had also left Ur behind. One day they came to the city of Babylon, which at that time was ruled by an evil king named Nimrûd. Nimrûd waged many wars, oppressed the people, and thought he was a god. He demanded that the people worship him.

The king even decided to build a huge tower that would reach up to the sky. He thought that if he could climb high enough, he could fight Allah (s.w.t.) and prove that he was the most powerful. Even before the tower was completed, Nimrûd climbed up and shot an arrow into the sky. He shouted to his people, "God is dead!"

Nimrûd had heard that a man named Ibrâhîm (a.s.) was in the city and was talking about a god whom he believed he had killed. The ruler was enraged by this and had Ibrâhîm (a.s.) brought to his palace.

When Ibrâhîm (a.s.) stood before Nimrûd, the ruler looked at him haughtily and said, "I have heard that you worship a god who gives and takes life. I am the most powerful god and I also have the power of life and death!" Ibrâhîm (a.s.) replied calmly, "There is only one true God, Allah (s.w.t.), who gives life and takes it away. He alone has power over everything."

To prove that he had the same abilities as Allah (s.w.t.), Nimrûd ordered a hundred prisoners to be brought to him. To fifty of them, he said, "You are free, you may go." Then he looked at the remaining fifty and ordered his guards, "Kill them."

Then he turned to Ibrâhîm (a.s.) again and said triumphantly, "You, see? I have given and taken life, just like your god."

Ibrâhîm (a.s.) shook his head and said, "Allah (s.w.t.) makes the sun rise in the east and set in the west. If you really have power, then let the sunrise in the west and set in the east."

Nimrûd was puzzled and annoyed, for he knew he could not do this. He could not control the sun. It was a lesson in humility, but Nimrûd refused to accept it. Instead of killing Ibrâhîm (a.s.), he had him expelled from the city. After all, Nimrûd was aware that he had not been able to kill God and feared His revenge if he harmed Ibrâhîm (a.s.).

One day, while his companions were setting up camp in a mountain, Ibrâhîm (a.s.) wandered around alone and thought. He looked up at the sky and began to talk to Allah (s.w.t.). He said, "O Allah (s.w.t.), I know that You have the power to raise the dead to life, but could You please show me how You do it? I just want to see it with my own eyes!"

Allah (s.w.t.) answered Ibrâhîm (a.s.) and asked, "Do you not have faith, Ibrâhîm (a.s.)?" He quickly replied, "Yes, my Lord, I have faith, but I just want to have more certainty in my heart."

Then Allah (s.w.t.) said to Ibrâhîm (a.s.), "Catch four birds and tame them so that they are close to you. Then put each of them on one of the mountains around you. Then call them and they will come to you quickly."

Ibrâhîm (a.s.) did exactly as Allah (s.w.t.) had told him. He took four birds, tamed them by feeding them and talking to them, and then put each bird on one of the surrounding mountains. Then he called them, and to his great surprise, the birds quickly flew to him! They sat on Ibrâhîm's (a.s.) shoulders. Then Allah (s.w.t.) said to him, "Birds are just like the souls of men. When their Creator calls them, they come." Ibrâhîm (a.s.) was deeply impressed and understood that Allah (s.w.t.) simply had to call the deceased to bring them back to life.

Then Ibrâhîm (a.s.), his nephew Lût (a.s.), and the others traveled on and finally arrived in a land known today as Palestine. Lût (a.s.) stayed with his family in a city called Sodom, while Ibrâhîm (a.s.) and the others moved on. They arrived in Egypt. The country was

one of the greatest civilizations at the time and was known for its impressive pyramids and large temples. Yet despite all their progress, the Egyptians still believed in many different gods. At this time, a powerful and ruthless king ruled the land. Ibrâhîm (a.s.) knew that this king was known for his greed and ruthlessness. As soon as he heard about beautiful women, he had them brought to him and kept them for himself.

Ibrâhîm (a.s.), who had heard about this, was afraid that the king would take his beautiful wife Sarah away from him when he saw her and kill him. So Ibrâhîm (a.s.) decided to pass Sarah off as his sister instead of his wife.

As Ibrâhîm (a.s.) had feared, when the king of Egypt heard of Sarah's beauty, he had her brought to his palace. But Sarah was a very clever woman. Before she was brought to the king, she prayed to Allah (s.w.t.) for protection and help.

While Sarah was in the palace, something amazing happened. Every time the king tried to approach her; he received a violent blow. The king was startled and understood that a higher power was protecting Sarah. He said to her, "Sarah, please, whatever this power is, tell it to leave me alone. I will not do anything to you!"

The king was hurt and begged Sarah to pray to her God so that he would recover. He promised her that he would never touch her again. So, Sarah prayed and Allah (s.w.t.) allowed the king to recover. Out of gratitude, the king let her go and even gave her gifts on the way. Princess Hajar recommended that the king give Sarah a slave and offered herself as one. She had already spoken to Ibrâhîm (a.s.) and Sarah and decided to worship only one god.

They left Egypt together and continued their journey.

The lesson from this story is that we should remain steadfast in our faith. A central message is an unwavering trust and devotion to Allah (s.w.t.). The conversation with Nimrûd, in which Ibrâhîm (a.s.) challenged the ruler to make the sun rise and set, shows the importance of defending beliefs and questioning what is accepted as true.

Sources: The Holy Qur'an, various hadiths, and Islamic traditions. Here are the sources from the Qur'an:

Sura 37, verses 83-99 | Sura 29, verses 16-17.

HADITH

قال رسول الله صلى الله عليه و سلم : الكريم، ابن الكريم، ابن الكريم، ابن الكريم، يوسف بن يعقوب بن إسحاق بن إبراهيم عليهم السلام

The Prophet Muhammad said: "The Noble One, the son of the Noble One, the son of the Noble One, the son of the Noble One, Yusuf, the son of Yaakub, the son of Is-haq, the son of Ibrâhîm, peace be upon them."

Sahih al-Bukhari 3390

DUA

PRAYER FOR PROTECTION FROM FALSE GODS

اللَّهُمَّ إِنِّي أَعُوذُ بِكَ أَنْ أُشْرِكَ بِكَ وَأَنَا أَعْلَمُ، وَأَسْتَغْفِرُكَ لِمَا أَعْلَمُ

Allāhumma inni a'ūdhu bika an ashrika bika wa-anä a'lamu, wa-astaghfiruka li-mä lä alam.

O Allah, I seek refuge in You, from knowingly committing evil against You, and I ask Your forgiveness for what I do not know.

Source: Ahmad
4/403

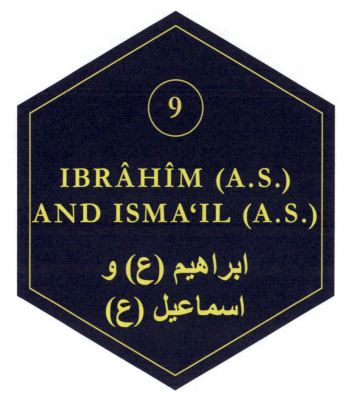

9

IBRÂHÎM (A.S.)
AND ISMA'IL (A.S.)

ابراهيم (ع) و
اسماعيل (ع)

IBRÂHÎM (A.S.) AND ISMA'IL (A.S.)

When Ibrâhîm (a.s.) and Sarah grew older, they were sad that they had no children. When Sarah suggested that Ibrâhîm (a.s.) take Hajar as his second wife, he agreed. Since Hajar also agreed, they married shortly afterwards. Not long after, their son, whom they named Isma'il (a.s.), was born.

But Sarah became jealous of Hajar and there were frequent quarrels. Allah (s.w.t.) spoke to Ibrâhîm (a.s.) and instructed him to take Hajar and her son Isma'il (a.s.) to the desert, to the area of present-day Mecca. Ibrâhîm (a.s.) was sad, but he trusted Allah (s.w.t.) and followed His instructions. He knew that Allah (s.w.t.) had a plan. So, he took Hajar and Isma'il (a.s.) to the desert and said to Hajar, "Hajar, I am leaving you and our baby here because Allah (s.w.t.) has commanded so. But don't be afraid, Allah (s.w.t.) will take care of you." Then he left.

The days in the desert were hard and lonely for Hajar and little Isma'il (a.s.), but Hajar was a strong and courageous woman. She ran back and forth between the hills of Safa and Marwa in search of water for her thirsty son. In her distress, she asked Allah (s.w.t.) for help.

And He answered Hajar's prayers. Suddenly, under the feet of little Isma'il (a.s.), a spring gushed forth. This was the spring of Zamzam, which is considered holy and blessed to this day.

Hajar drank with relief, quenched the thirst of Isma'il (a.s.), and filled their water hoses. Shortly afterwards, a caravan of travelers passed by. When they discovered that there was fresh water, they asked Hajar for permission to drink from it. She allowed them to drink and fill their hoses. Some even settled nearby, and soon a community grew up around the spring.

Soon after, Ibrâhîm (a.s.) returned to Hajar and his son. Ibrâhîm (a.s.) had a dream in which Allah (s.w.t.) said to him, "Ibrâhîm (a.s.), I want you to bring your son Isma'il (a.s.) as a sacrifice." Ibrâhîm (a.s.) woke up and was sad, but he knew that he had to obey Allah (s.w.t.). He went to Isma'il (a.s.) and said with tearful eyes, "My dear son, I had a dream in which Allah (s.w.t.) told me that I must sacrifice you. I am very sad, but we must do what He tells us to do."

Isma'il (a.s.) was courageous and replied, "Father, if this is what Allah (s.w.t.) wants, then I am ready. I trust you and I trust Allah (s.w.t.)."

So, the two of them set off for a mountain because Ibrâhîm (a.s.) wanted to sacrifice his son there. As they approached the mountain, a jinn suddenly appeared. He said deceitfully, "Ibrâhîm (a.s.), what are you doing? You should not sacrifice your son! That cannot be right!" But Ibrâhîm (a.s.) realized that this jinn was trying to dissuade him from doing what Allah (s.w.t.) had told him to do. He took some stones and threw them at the jinn to drive him away.

"Get lost!" Ibrâhîm (a.s.) shouted. "I will do what Allah (s.w.t.) has told me to do and I will not listen to your lies!" The jinn disappeared and Ibrâhîm (a.s.) and Isma'il (a.s.) continued on their way until they reached the place where Ibrâhîm (a.s.) was ready to make the sacrifice.

Isma'il (a.s.), brave and trusting, said, "Father, if this is the will of Allah (s.w.t.), then I am ready. May He be pleased with you." Ibrâhîm (a.s.), with tears in his eyes, raised his knife and said, "O Allah (s.w.t.), I am doing this only because You have commanded me to. Please protect my son."

At that moment, they heard a voice from heaven, "Ibrâhîm (a.s.)! You have proved your faith!" Ibrâhîm (a.s.) looked around with relief and noticed a large sheep nearby. They sacrificed it in thanksgiving to Allah (s.w.t.) and shared the meat with the poor and needy.

The story of Ibrâhîm (a.s.) and Isma'il (a.s.) is often narrated as an example of devotion, faith, and obedience to the will of Allah (s.w.t.). It is also the origin of the festival of Eid al-Adha, also known as the Feast of Sacrifice, in which Muslims around the world sacrifice sheep and share the meat with the needy to commemorate Ibrâhîm (a.s.) and Isma'il (a.s.).

This story teaches us that we should always trust in Allah (s.w.t.) even if we do not understand his plans. We should be as brave and steadfast as Hajar and Isma'il (a.s.) were. History shows us that obedience to Allah (s.w.t.), even in the most challenging times, is always rewarded and how important it is to always be grateful and share our blessings with others.

Sources: The Holy Qur'an:

Sura 14, verse 37 | Sura 37, verses 102-111.

HADITH

قال ابن عباس: كانت رؤيا الأنبياء وحيًا

Ibn Abbas said: "The dreams of the prophets were a form of revelation."

Al-Mustadrak 3613 and Al-Albani in Dhilal al-Jannah 463

DUA

PRAYER FOR SUPPORT AND GUIDANCE

رَبِّ أَعِنِّي وَلَا تُعِنْ عَلَيَّ، وَانْصُرْنِي وَلَا تَنْصُرْ عَلَيَّ، وَامْكُرْ لِي وَلَا تَمْكُرْ عَلَيَّ، وَاهْدِنِي وَيَسِّرْ هُدَايَ إِلَيَّ، وَانْصُرْنِي عَلَى مَنْ بَغَى عَلَيَّ، اللَّهُمَّ اجْعَلْنِي لَكَ شَاكِرًا، لَكَ ذَاكِرًا، لَكَ رَاهِبًا، لَكَ مِطْوَاعًا إِلَيْكَ، مُخْبِتًا، أَوْ مُنِيبًا، رَبِّ تَقَبَّلْ تَوْبَتِي، وَاغْسِلْ حَوْبَتِي، وَأَجِبْ دَعْوَتِي، وَثَبِّتْ حُجَّتِي، وَاهْدِ قَلْبِي، وَسَدِّدْ لِسَانِي، وَاسْلُلْ سَخِيمَةَ قَلْبِي

Rabbi a'inni wala tu'in 'alayya, wansurni wala tansur 'alayya, wamkur li wala tamkur 'alayya, wahdini wa yassir hudaaya ilayya, wansurni 'alaa man bagha 'alayya. Allahumma ij'alni laka shaakiran, laka zaakiran, laka raahiban, laka muti'an ilayka, mukhbitan aw muniban. Rabbi taqabbal tawbati, wa ghsil hawbati, wa ajib da'wati, wa thabbit hujjati, wahdi qalbi, wasdidd lisaani, waslul sakhiimata qalbi.

Source: Jami` at-Tirmidhi 3551

O Allah, help me and do not help against me, support me and do not support against me, plot for me and do not plot against me, guide me and make my guidance easy for me. Help me against those who transgress against me. O Allah, make me grateful to You, mindful of You, reverent towards You, obedient to You, humble before You, penitent, or constantly turning to You in repentance. O Allah, accept my repentance, wash away my sins, answer my supplication, establish my proof, guide my heart, make my tongue true, and remove the hatred from my heart.

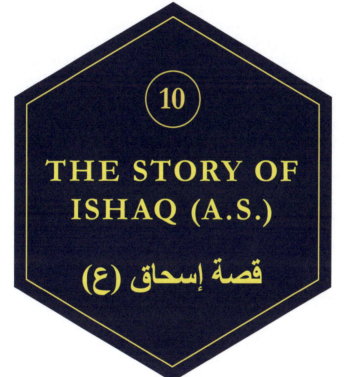

10

THE STORY OF ISHAQ (A.S.)

قصة إسحاق (ع)

THE STORY OF ISHAQ (A.S.)

Once upon a time, a long, long time ago, the Prophet Ibrâhîm (a.s.) and his wife Sarah were still living in Canaan. Their greatest wish was to have a child, but despite their prayers, they remained childless. One day, when Ibrâhîm (a.s.) received guests, they were not ordinary people. They were angels sent by Allah (s.w.t.) and they brought astonishing news. They announced that Sarah would have a son!

Sarah was surprised and could hardly believe it. She asked, "How can I have a child when I am so old, and my husband has also reached an advanced age?" But the angels replied, "This is Allah's (s.w.t.) plan. Do not question His intention, for He does what He wills."

Then the angels announced that they had received the order from Allah (s.w.t.) to destroy the city of Sodom. The people of Sodom were bad and unjust, so Allah (s.w.t.) decided to punish them. Ibrâhîm (a.s.) was worried about his nephew Lût (a.s.) who lived in Sodom. However, the angels assured him that the righteous would not be punished and set off for Sodom.

Not long after, just as the angels had predicted, Sarah gave birth to a son. They named him Ishāq (a.s.). Sarah and Ibrâhîm (a.s.) were overjoyed. They had waited a long time for this moment and were deeply grateful to Allah (s.w.t.) for His mercy.

When Ishaq (a.s.) grew older, he grew up to be a God-fearing man, just like his father Ibrahim and his brother Isma'il (a.s.). He followed the path of Allah (s.w.t.) and taught others to do good and pay homage to Allah (s.w.t.). Ishāq (a.s.) became a father himself. He named his son Yaqûb (a.s.). Yaqûb (a.s.) later became the father of the Bani Israel, the twelve tribes of Israel. Isma'il (a.s.) became the father of the Arabs. In this way, Allah's (s.w.t.)

promise to Ibrâhîm (a.s.) that he would be the father of many nations was fulfilled.

The story of Ishāq (a.s.) teaches us that Allah (s.w.t.) answers the prayers of those who are patient and steadfast and that even the seemingly impossible is possible. It shows us that God's ways are beyond our understanding. We must have faith in His plan and know that He always wants the best for us.

> **Sources:** The Holy Qur'an:
>
> Sura 11, verse 69-73 | Sura 21, verse 72 | Sura 37, verse 112.

HADITH

كان النَّبيُّ صلَّى الله عليه وسلَّم يُعوِّذُ حسَنًا وحُسينًا: (أُعيذُكما بكلماتِ اللهِ التَّامَّةِ مِن كلِّ شيطانٍ وهامَّةٍ ومِن كلِّ عينٍ لامَّةٍ) ثمَّ يقولُ صلَّى الله عليه وسلَّم: كان إبراهيمُ صلواتُ اللهِ عليه يُعوِّذُ به ابنَيْهِ إسماعيلَ وإسحاقَ

Prophet Muhammad asked for divine protection for Hassan and Hussein by saying, "I place you under the protection of the perfect words of Allah, from every devil, from every harmful creature, and every evil eye." Then he added: "Ibrâhîm, peace be upon him, used the same words to protect his sons Ishmael and Ishaq."

Sahih Ibn Hibban 1012 and
Sahih al-Bukhari 3371

DUA

PRAYER FOR HAPPINESS AND PROSPERITY

اللهم قَنِعني بِما رزقتَني وبارك لِي فِيه واخْلُف علي كُل غَائِبةٍ بِخيرٍ

Allahumma, qannini bima razaqtani wa barik li fihi wa khluf 'alayya kulla ghaa'ibatin bikhayr.

O Allah, content me with what You have provided for me, bless it for me, and replace any loss with something better.

Source:
Al-Adab
Al-Mufrad 681

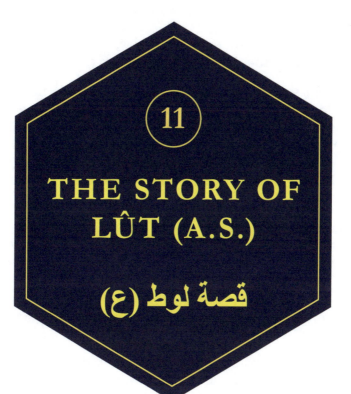

11

THE STORY OF LÛT (A.S.)

قصة لوط (ع)

THE STORY OF LÛT (A.S.)

Lût (a.s.), the nephew of Ibrâhîm (a.s.), lived in a city called Sodom, where the people were bad and disobedient to Allah (s.w.t.). They did not treat each other well, were mean to travelers, and had other habits that displeased Allah (s.w.t.).

Lût (a.s.) was sad about this and kept saying to the people, "Why do you do such bad things? Allah (s.w.t.) does not like this. He wants us to be nice to each other and respect each other. You should help travelers instead of cheating them. You will have to do better." But the people of Sodom only laughed at Lût (a.s.) and said, "Lût (a.s.), you are just a human being like us. Why should we listen to you?"

One day, some beautiful people came to Lût (a.s.). They looked like ordinary travelers, but they were angels sent by Allah (s.w.t.). Do you remember the angels who visited Ibrâhîm (a.s.) and Sarah before? They had moved on to Sodom and came to Lût (a.s.). He was a good host and invited the strangers in. The wicked people in the city noticed that Lût (a.s.) had a visitor and they wanted to harm the strangers.

Lût (a.s.) was very worried and called out to the people standing outside his door, "These guests are under my protection. Please do not harm them." But the people of Sodom did not listen to him. They banged on the door and windows and prepared to enter Lût's (a.s.) house.

At that moment, the angels revealed their true identity and said to Lût (a.s.), "Do not be afraid, Lût (a.s.). Allah (s.w.t.) has sent us to punish this city. You and your family must leave the city that night before dawn; but be careful, don't look back when you leave."

Lût (a.s.) and his family did as they were told and left the city secretly. They did not look back, just as the angels had instructed them to do. When hot stones rained down on Sodom from the sky in an incredible roar and covered the city, Lût's (a.s.) wife looked back. Even as she looked back, she froze into a pillar of salt. Lût (a.s.) and the others were able to escape to a safe place. Sodom was destroyed and with it the evil inhabitants.

The story of Lût (a.s.) teaches us that we must obey Allah (s.w.t.) and his prophets. It shows us that bad behavior has consequences and that it is important to be respectful and kind to our fellow human beings and to always treat our guests well.

Sources: The Holy Qur'an:

Sura 11, verses 77-83 | Sura 26, verses 160-175 | Sura 7, verses 80-84 | Sura 51, verses 31-37 | Sura 54, verses 33-39.

HADITH

قال رسول الله صلى الله عليه و سلم: إن أخوف ما أخاف على أمتي، عمل قوم لوط

The Prophet Muhammad said: "What I fear most for my community are the deeds of the people of Lût."

Al-Albani, Sahih al-Jami' 1552

DUA

PRAYER TO CONFIRM THE TRUTH

رَبِّ ٱحْكُم بِٱلْحَقِّ وَرَبُّنَا ٱلرَّحْمَٰنُ ٱلْمُسْتَعَانُ عَلَىٰ مَا تَصِفُونَ

Rabbi ḥkum bi-l-ḥaqqi wa-rabbunā r-raḥmānu l-mustaʿānu ʿalā mā taṣifūna.

My Lord, judge in truth. And our Lord is the All-Merciful, Whose help is to be invoked against what you claim.

Source: Sura
Al-Anbya
(21:112)

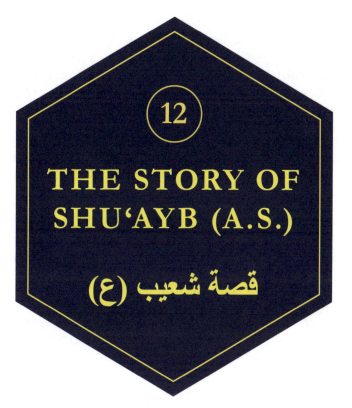

12

THE STORY OF SHU'AYB (A.S.)

قصة شعيب (ع)

THE STORY OF SHU'AYB (A.S.)

The Prophet Shu'ayb (a.s.) was born in a town called Madyan, located in present-day Jordan. The people of Madyan were not fair in their business dealings and often cheated others. They deliberately weighed and measured their goods incorrectly to make more profit. They treated the poor badly and had no fear of the consequences of their actions. They even attacked travelers and robbed them of their belongings.

When Shu'ayb (a.s.) grew up, he noticed the unjust behavior of the people of Madyan, and this saddened him. Allah (s.w.t.), the All-Knowing and Merciful, sent him as His Prophet to teach the people of Madyan and guide them to righteousness.

Shu'ayb (a.s.) said to the people of Madyan, "O my people! Fear Allah (s.w.t.) and be fair and just in your dealings. Do not deceive people! Treat the poor with respect and kindness. Allah (s.w.t.) is All-Knowing and sees everything you do."

The people of Madyan only laughed and made fun of Shu'ayb (a.s.). They refused to listen to his advice, continued to treat the poor badly, and cheated and robbed travelers in their businesses.

Shu'ayb (a.s.) though did not give up, he prayed to Allah (s.w.t.) and said, "O Allah (s.w.t.), give guidance to these people and show them the right path." But the rich and arrogant people in the city only laughed. One of them said loudly, "Ha! Shu'ayb (a.s.), you talk too much! If you are so clever, why don't you show us all the gold and silver you have?"

Shu'ayb (a.s.) replied calmly, "Wealth is not the most important thing in life. It is more important to have a good heart and help each other."

The arrogant inhabitants of Madyan then warned the righteous among them, "If you follow Shu'ayb (a.s.), you will be as poor and insignificant as he is!"

Shu'ayb (a.s.) continued, "The wealth you have amassed was obtained through injustice and deceit. Remember that no amount of gold or silver can redeem you from your evil deeds!" One of the rich men stepped forward and said mockingly, "Ah Shu'ayb (a.s.), do you really think that your talk impresses us? We have money, and with it, we can have anything we want!"

Shu'ayb (a.s.) looked at the man sadly and said, "But can you buy love, respect, and the blessings of Allah (s.w.t.) with it? True happiness is not found in riches, but in a pure heart and in serving Allah (s.w.t.) and our fellow human beings. Please, dear friends, change before it is too late. He sees everything we do."

The people of Madyan did not listen to him. They even toyed with the idea of killing Shu'ayb (a.s.). And so it happened that Allah punished them (s.w.t.) - just like the other peoples who had defied His word and mocked His messengers. A terrible earthquake caused all the houses in the city to tremble and collapse. The unjust people who had built their wealth on the suffering of others found their graves under the ruins. Shu'ayb (a.s.), together with some righteous people, had escaped from the city and reached safety.

The story of Shu'ayb (a.s.) teaches us that we should always be just and honest in our dealings. We should neither steal nor cheat and respect the poor and be kind to them. For Allah (s.w.t.) sees everything we do and will reward or punish us for it. Each of us has the choice of doing the right thing or the wrong thing.

Sources: Holy Qur'an:

Sura 7, verses 85-93 | Sura 11, verses 84-95.

HADITH

سَمِعْتُ رَسُولَ اللهِ صَلَّى اللَّهُ عليه وسلَّمَ يقولُ: يُؤْتَى بالرَّجُلِ يَومَ القِيَامَةِ، فيُلْقَى في النَّارِ، فَتَنْدَلِقُ أَقْتَابُ بَطْنِهِ، فَيَدُورُ بها كما يَدُورُ الحِمَارُ بالرَّحَى، فَيَجْتَمِعُ إلَيْهِ أَهْلُ النَّارِ، فيقولونَ: يا فُلَانُ ما لَكَ؟ أَلَمْ تَكُنْ تَأْمُرُ بالمَعروفِ، وَتَنْهَى عَنِ المُنْكَرِ؟ فيقولُ: بَلَى، قَدْ كُنْتُ آمُرُ بالمَعروفِ وَلَا آتِيهِ، وَأَنْهَى عَنِ المُنْكَرِ وَآتِيهِ

I heard the Messenger of Allah say: "A man will be brought forward on the Day of Judgment and thrown into the Fire. His belly will be torn apart, and he will circle his intestines as a donkey would circle an oil mill. The inhabitants of hell will come to him and say: 'What has brought you here? He will answer, 'Yes, it was me. I commanded what was good, but I did not do it myself, and I disapproved of what was bad, but I did it myself."

Sahih Muslim 2989 and Sahih
al-Bukhari 3267

DUA

PRAYER FOR THE FOR PROTECTION FROM IGNORANCE

أَعُوذُ بِٱللَّهِ أَنْ أَكُونَ مِنَ ٱلْجَٰهِلِينَ

A'oodhu billahi an akoona min al-jahileen.

I seek refuge in Allah from being among the ignorant.

Source: Surat
(al-Baqara)
2:67

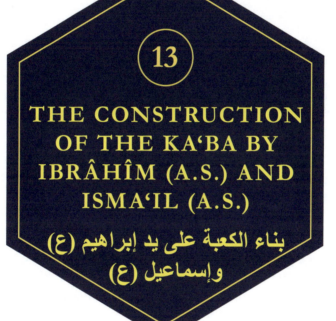

13

THE CONSTRUCTION OF THE KA'BA BY IBRÂHÎM (A.S.) AND ISMA'IL (A.S.)

بناء الكعبة على يد إبراهيم (ع) وإسماعيل (ع)

THE CONSTRUCTION OF THE KA'BA BY IBRÂHÎM (A.S.) AND ISMA'IL (A.S.)

Do you remember Isma'il (a.s.), the son of Ibrâhîm (a.s.)? In the meantime, a real city had grown up around the spring of Zamzam, where Isma'il (a.s.) and his mother had previously been left by Ibrâhîm (a.s.). This city bears the name Mecca and is still there today.

Ibrâhîm (a.s.) and Isma'il (a.s.) lived together in Mecca for a while. One day, Ibrâhîm (a.s.) received a message from Allah (s.w.t.). He said, "Ibrâhîm (a.s.), I have a great task for you and your son Isma'il (a.s.). I want you both to erect a special building in Mecca. It shall be called the Ka'ba and will be a place of prayer for all people."

Ibrâhîm (a.s.) looked at Isma'il (a.s.) and announced happily, "My dear son, Allah (s.w.t.) has given us a very important task! He wants us to build a house of prayer for Him here, in this place. It will be a place where people from all over the world will come to pray undisturbed and in peace."

Isma'il's (a.s.) eyes lit up with excitement. "Father, this is wonderful! I will help you!" he replied eagerly. And so, they got to work. They collected large stones, worked them, and laid them carefully on top of each other in the center of the city. As they worked, they prayed and thanked Allah (s.w.t.) for this honorable task.

Ibrâhîm (a.s.) prayed, "O our Lord, accept this from us, for You are the All-Hearing, the All-Knowing." Then the two prayed together, "Our Lord, make us both devoted to You and our offspring a community devoted to You. And show us our rites and accept our repentance, for You are the Acceptor of Repentance, the Merciful." Further they prayed, "Our Lord, send to the people a messenger from among them who will read Your signs to them, teach them the Scriptures, and purify them. Verily, You are the Exalted, the Wise."

When Ibrâhîm (a.s.) and Isma'il (a.s.) had almost finished building the Ka'ba, the moment came when they needed a special stone. This was to be a special symbol for the sanctuary.

While they were thinking about what to do, the angel Jibril appeared with a beautiful stone sent down from heaven. It was the Black Stone, Hajar al-Aswad. It is said that the stone was initially as white as milk and symbolized purity and divinity. However, the sins of the people over the centuries had turned the stone black.

Jibrīl explained to Ibrâhîm (a.s.) that this stone was a gift from Allah (s.w.t.) and that it should be placed at the eastern corner of the Ka'ba. Ibrâhîm (a.s.) was grateful and accepted the stone. He summoned his son Isma'il (a.s.) and together they placed the Black Stone in the Ka'ba. As they placed the stone, they asked Allah (s.w.t.) for His blessings. The Black Stone became a central element of the Ka'ba and later an important part of the Hajj rituals, where pilgrims try to touch or kiss the stone as an expression of their deep love and devotion to Allah (s.w.t.).

The lesson of this story: This story teaches us the importance of family. Ibrâhîm (a.s.) and Isma'il (a.s.) worked together to build the Ka'ba and supported each other. This shows the importance of sticking together as a family and supporting each other. It also teaches us the sanctity of the Ka'ba as a place of worship. By building the Ka'ba, Ibrâhîm (a.s.) and Isma'il (a.s.) followed the command of Allah (s.w.t.) and created a place that is a center of faith for all Muslims.

Sources: The Holy Qur'an:

Sura 2, verses 127-129 | Sura 22, verses 26-27.

HADITH

روي عن ابن عباس عن رسول الله أنه قال: «لما فرغ إبراهيم من بناء
البيت أمره الله عز وجل أن ينادي في الحج، فقام على المقام، فقال: يا
أيها الناس إن ربكم قد بنى بيتًا فحجوه، وأجيبوا الله عز وجل، فأجابوه
في أصلاب الرجال وأرحام النساء: أجبناك، أجبناك، أجبناك، اللهم
لبيك»، قال: فكل من حج اليوم فهو ممن أجاب إبراهيم على قدر ما لبى

It is reported from Ibn 'Abbas that the Prophet said: "After he had finished building the Kaaba, Allah, may He be exalted, ordered him and Ibrâhîm to call the
people to pilgrimage. Ibrâhîm stood on the podium and said, 'O people, Allah
has built a house, so perform the pilgrimage to this house. Follow the invitation
of Allah, exalted is He. The people responded by saying, 'We respond to Your call,
O Allah, we respond to Your call.' They uttered the words 'Labbaik, Allahumma,
Labbaik' (Here we are, O Allah, here we are). The Prophet explained that anyone
who performs the pilgrimage in this way, responding as Ibrahim did, is considered
to have responded to Ibrahim's invitation."

Al-Hakim in Al-Mustadrak
2/389 and Al-Bayhaqi in
As-Sunan 5/176

DUA

PRAYER FOR SUPPORT AGAINST THE DISBELIEVERS

رَبَّنَا تُؤَاخِذْنَا إِن نَّسِينَا أَوْ أَخْطَأْنَا رَبَّنَا وَلَا تَحْمِلْ عَلَيْنَا إِصْرًا كَمَا حَمَلْتَهُ
عَلَى الَّذِينَ مِن قَبْلِنَا رَبَّنَا وَلَا تُحَمِّلْنَا مَا لَا طَاقَةَ لَنَا بِهِ وَاعْفُ عَنَّا وَاغْفِرْ
لَنَا وَارْحَمْنَا أَنتَ مَوْلَانَا فَانصُرْنَا عَلَى الْقَوْمِ الْكَافِرِينَ

Rabbanā lā tu'āḫiḏnā 'in nasīnā
'aw 'aḫṭa'nā rabbanā wa-lā taḥmil
'alaynā 'iṣran ka-mā ḥamaltahū
'alā llaḏīna min qablinā rabbanā
wa-lā tuḥammilnā mā lā ṭāqata
lanā bihī wa-'fu 'annā wa-ġfir
lanā wa-rḥamnā 'anta mawlānā
fa-nṣurnā 'alā l-qawmi l-kāfirīna.

Source: Surat
Al-Baqarah
(2:286)

Our Lord do not reproach us if
we forget or make mistakes.
Our Lord do not impose on us a
burden as You imposed on those
before us. Our Lord, and do not
burden us with anything for which
we have no strength. And forgive
us, pardon us, and have mercy
on us. You are our protector. So,
help us against the people of the
unbelievers!

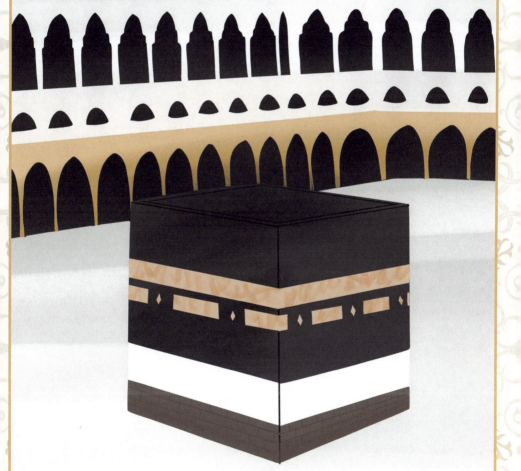

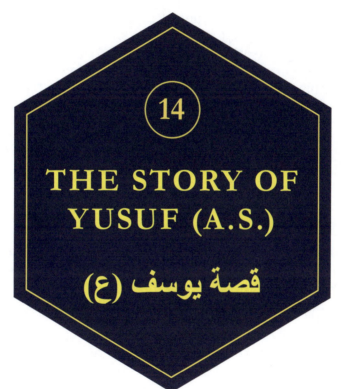

14

THE STORY OF
YUSUF (A.S.)

قصة يوسف (ع)

THE STORY OF YUSUF (A.S.)

A young man named Yusuf (a.s.) lived with his father Yaqûb (a.s.) and his eleven brothers. Do you remember Yaqûb (a.s.)? He was the son of Isḥâq (a.s.). Yusuf (a.s.), the grandson of Isḥâq (a.s.) and the great-grandson of Ibrâhîm (a.s.) was no ordinary boy - he was very clever, polite, and always ready to help. This impressed his father very much. "Yusuf (a.s.), my son," Yaqûb (a.s.) often said, "you are truly a blessing to our family. Your brothers could learn so much from you."

Instead of learning from Yusuf (a.s.), these words filled his brothers with jealousy. They did not like the fact that their father praised Yusuf more and paid more attention to him than to them. Yaqûb (a.s.) also held his youngest son in high esteem, but all the others were jealous.

One day, Yusuf (a.s.) told his father about a strange dream he had. "Father," said Yusuf (a.s.) excitedly, "I had a strange dream. I saw eleven stars, the sun, and the moon, and they all bowed down to me. What can this mean?"

Yaqûb (a.s.) smiled and stroked his son's head lovingly. "My dear Yusuf (a.s.)," he replied, "this is a sign that Allah (s.w.t.) has great plans for you. You will be a great man one day, and even your brothers will show you, their respect. Don't tell this dream to anyone, especially your brothers, because they might become jealous and want to harm you."

Nevertheless, the jealousy of the brothers of Yusuf (a.s.) grew. They could not bear the fact that their father favored Yusuf (a.s.) because he was clever and good-natured. In their jealousy, they decided to get rid of their brother. They excitedly asked their father, "Father, may we take Yusuf (a.s.) with us to play outside and have fun? We will take good care of him!" Their father was worried and said, "Oh, I'm afraid something might happen to him. He's still so young." But the brothers begged and pleaded that they would look after him. Finally, the father gave in and let Yusuf (a.s.) go with his brothers.

The sun was shining as they played outside, but Yusuf's (a.s.) brothers had no fun in mind. They took Yusuf (a.s.) and deceitfully threw him into a dry well. Poor Yusuf (a.s.) cried out, "Help! Why are you doing this? Get me up again!" But his brothers did not heed his cries.

Then they came up with an idea. They took Yusuf's (a.s.) beautiful robe and dipped it in the blood of a sheep they had killed earlier. When they got home, they held up the bloody robe and said with sad faces, "Father, we have found Yusuf's (a.s.) robe. A wild animal must have caught him!" Their father was sad and wept for his beloved son, but he sensed that something was wrong. He said with tears in his eyes "No, my sons, something tells me that you are not telling the truth, but Allah (s.w.t.) will help me and I will be patient."

The next day, Yusuf (a.s.) was still trapped in the well. He was very thirsty. But suddenly he heard noises from above. It was merchants on their way to the city. They lowered their bucket into the well to draw water, but instead of water, they found Yusuf (a.s.)! The merchants were astonished.

Just at that moment, Yusuf's (a.s.) brothers came back from the pasture and saw what was happening. They went to the merchants and said, "This is our brother, but we have too many mouths to feed at home. You can have him for a few silver coins." The merchants did not hesitate and bought Yusuf (a.s.) for a low price. Yusuf's (a.s.) brothers were happy to be rid of him at last.

The merchants took Yusuf (a.s.) to Egypt and sold him there to a rich man named Azîz. Yusuf now far away from his homeland and his family, quickly learned the foreign language. Azîz was a rich and powerful man and he soon noticed how clever and hard-working Yusuf was. One day Azîz said to Yusuf, "Yusuf (a.s.), you are a very clever and trustworthy boy, I will make you the

caretaker of my house!" Yusuf (a.s.) felt honored by his words and worked even harder.

Then there was a problem - Azîz's wife Sulaikha. She tried to seduce the handsome Yusuf (a.s.). Yusuf, however, refused because he was a righteous young man who would never have betrayed Azîz.

While Yusuf (a.s.) wanted to flee the room quickly, Sulaikha tore at his shirt and tore it from behind. Just at that moment, Azîz entered the room and saw the torn shirt of Yusuf (a.s.). Sulaikha exclaimed, "What should be the punishment for someone who wanted to harm your family? Shouldn't he be imprisoned or given a severe punishment?"

But Yusuf (a.s.) said, "It was she who wanted to seduce me!"

A wise family member suggested that they look at the torn shirt as proof. If Yusuf's shirt was torn from the front, he would have lied, but since it was torn from the back, he had to tell the truth. Azîz saw the torn shirt and understood the truth. He said to Yusuf (a.s.), "Overlook what has happened." And to Sulaikha he said, "Ask forgiveness for your sin because you lied and thus did something wrong."

But the story spread quickly in the city. The ladies of the town talked about Sulaikha and said, "The nobleman's wife is trying to seduce her slave!"

Sulaikha heard the gossip and mockery and decided to invite the ladies of the city to a meeting. She gave them each a knife and a fruit and then invited Yusuf (a.s.) to come in. The ladies were so stunned by Yusuf's (a.s.) beauty that they accidentally cut their hands while peeling the fruit. Then Sulaikha said, "Look, this is the man you blame me for! Yes, I tried to seduce him, but he persisted. I would like to have him thrown into prison."

And so it happened that the sincere Yusuf (a.s.) was sent to prison. Azîz agreed to this because he wanted the scandal surrounding his wife to die down.

Yet even in this dark place, Yusuf (a.s.) continued to show his kindness and wisdom. The prison guards noticed this and treated him with respect. He helped other prisoners and told them about Allah (s.w.t.). Two fellow prisoners told Yusuf about their strange dreams.

One of the men, who had previously worked as a baker, told Yusuf (a.s.), "I dreamt that I was carrying bread on my head and the birds were eating it. What can this mean?"

The other man, who was the Pharaoh's former cupbearer, said, "In my dream, I was pressing wine. What does that mean, Yusuf?"

Yusuf (a.s.), who had the gift of interpreting dreams, told the first man, "Unfortunately, your dream means that you will be executed, and the birds will eat from your head." He told the second man, "Your dream is a good sign! You will be released and serve wine for Pharaoh again." Yusuf (a.s.) asked him to remember him and tell Pharaoh about him when he returned to his service. But the man forgot Yusuf (a.s.) when he was released from prison.

A few years passed, and one day Pharaoh himself had a strange dream that no one could interpret. Then the former prison inmate, who had become Pharaoh's cupbearer again, remembered Yusuf (a.s.) and told Pharaoh about him. He had Yusuf (a.s.) taken out of prison and told him about his dream in which seven lean cows ate seven fat cows and seven green ears of corn were devoured by seven thin ears of corn.

Yusuf (a.s.) interpreted the dream and told Pharaoh, "There will be seven years of abundance followed by seven years of drought. You must make provisions in the good years to have enough in the bad years."

Yusuf's (a.s.) wisdom impressed the Pharaoh and appointed him a high official in charge of Egypt's storehouses. Yusuf (a.s.) had stocks built up and so it was that the Egyptians had enough to eat even in times of drought.

But the supplies in many parts of the region, including the land where Yusuf's (a.s.) family lived, had run out. Yusuf's (a.s.) brothers, still unaware of what had happened to their brother, set off for Egypt because they had heard that grain was available there.

When the brothers arrived in Egypt, they were sent to Yusuf (a.s.). Yet even when they had him right in front of them, they did not recognize their brother, but he knew very well that his brothers were standing in front of him, though he did not reveal his identity. The brothers introduced themselves to Yusuf (a.s.) as honest people who had come from a distant land to buy grain. Yusuf (a.s.) wanted to test their honesty and see if they had changed since they had thrown him into the well as a child. He handed them the grain they had bought. Then he said to his brothers, "Look, I have given you the full measure of grain and I am hospitable to you. The next time you come, bring your youngest brother with you so that I know that you are not cheats or spies." Yusuf (a.s.) said this because he wanted to see his youngest brother again, whom he missed very much.

To make sure that the brothers would return and take the youngest with them next time, Yusuf (a.s.) hid the money with which the brothers had paid for the grain in the sacks of grain. Yusuf (a.s.) had done this out of brotherly love and compassion. He wanted to ensure that his family had enough resources to provide for their needs. Also, this was part of his plan to test their character.

When the brothers arrived at their home, Yaqûb (a.s.) initially did not want them to take the youngest with them on their next journey to Egypt. Eventually, he agreed, as they needed more grain and the kind stranger had even given them back the money for their purchase.

So, the brothers set off on their journey again. When they arrived in Egypt, Yusuf (a.s.) took his youngest brother aside and revealed his identity to him. He told him that he was Yusuf (a.s.), but that he should keep it a secret.

Yusuf (a.s.) wanted to test his brothers again and see whether they had changed. So, he devised a plan. He secretly had a silver cup placed in his youngest brother's grain sack. As they were about to leave Egypt, they were stopped by soldiers, searched, and accused of stealing the cup. When the cup was found in the youngest brother's sack, the other brothers asked that he be spared and offered to stay in Egypt instead.

Together with the soldiers, the 11 brothers returned to Egypt. The older brothers first said to Yusuf (a.s.) that if the youngest had stolen, he should receive the just punishment for it, and they distanced themselves from him. Yusuf (a.s.) explained that according to the law, the one in whose possession the cup was found must remain in Egypt as punishment. Since it was their youngest brother, the older brothers were in a difficult position because they had promised their father Yaqûb (a.s.) to bring him back home safely.

Then one of the elder brothers stepped forward and said to Yusuf (a.s.), "O noble Lord, he has an old father who is very attached to him. Why don't you take one of us in his place, for we see that you are a kind person?" Yusuf (a.s.) replied, "Allah (s.w.t.) protects us from punishing anyone except the one from whom we found the stolen goods. Otherwise, it would be unjust."

The brothers were desperate because they knew how much their father would suffer. They discussed among themselves, and the eldest among them decided that he would stay in Egypt and accompany the youngest until their father allowed him to return.

When the brothers returned home, they were very anxious to tell their father Yaqûb the news that they had returned without his beloved youngest son. As they stood before Yaqûb, they said in trembling voices, "O father, your son has stolen, and we can only testify to what we know. We saw that he was carrying a valuable cup. We could not have foreseen this."

Yaqûb was deeply saddened, and his eyes filled with tears. He said, "No, your souls have deceived you. Patience is in order. May Allah (s.w.t.) bring him back to me. He is the All-Knowing, the Wise."

He then turned away and began to cry quietly. He said, "Oh, how much I miss Yusuf (a.s.)!" and his eyes became cloudy with grief, he could no longer see anything and was completely depressed. Deep in his heart, Yaqûb (a.s.) was convinced that Yusuf (a.s.) was alive and that his youngest son was not a thief. He finally decided to send his sons to Egypt again to search for their younger brother. Before they left, he gave them advice and spoke to them with wisdom and hope. He said, "O my sons, go and search for Yusuf (a.s.) and his brother, and do not doubt Allah's (s.w.t.) mercy, for no one doubts Allah's (s.w.t.) mercy except the disbelieving people."

So, the brothers set off for Egypt again. When they arrived there, they went to Yusuf (a.s.) and asked him urgently for more grain. They also told him about the difficulties of their family and how desperate their old father Yaqûb (a.s.) was. Yusuf (a.s.) was moved when he heard about his father's sadness. He could no longer keep his identity a secret and said to his brothers, "Do you know what you did to Yusuf (a.s.) and his brother when you were ignorant?"

The brothers were astonished and wondered how he knew Yusuf (a.s.). They finally asked him, "Are you Yusuf (a.s.)?" He (a.s.) replied with a smile, "Yes, I am your brother. Allah (s.w.t.) has indeed done us good."

The brothers realized their mistakes and asked Yusuf (a.s.) for forgiveness. They realized that he held a high position and that they were now in his debt. Yusuf (a.s.) forgave them and asked them to take his shirt and put it on the face of their father Yaqûb (a.s.) so that he could regain his sight.

When the brothers returned home and put the shirt over Yaqûb's (a.s.) face, he could see again. He knew that Allah (s.w.t.) had answered his prayers and was overjoyed that his beloved son Yusuf (a.s.) was still alive.

Eventually, the entire family made their way to Egypt to meet Yusuf (a.s.). He welcomed them warmly. He gave them a large house and made sure that they wanted for nothing. Yusuf (a.s.) said to Yaqûb (a.s.), "O my father, this is the interpretation of my earlier dream. My Lord has made it come true."

Shortly before Yaqûb (a.s.) died, he turned to his sons and asked, "What will you worship after my death?" They replied, "We will worship your God and the God of your fathers, Ibrâhîm (a.s.), Isma'il (a.s.) and Ishâq (a.s.), the only God, and we will surrender to Him."

The story of Yusuf (a.s.) and Yaqûb (a.s.) teaches us that we should always trust Allah (s.w.t.). It also shows the importance of forgiveness and reconciliation, as Yusuf (a.s.) forgave his brothers despite their ill-treatment of him. It also teaches us to stick to moral principles, even if it is not always easy.

Sources: The Holy Qur'an:

Sura 2, verse 133 | Sura 12, verses 3-102.

HADITH

وَرَوَى الْبَيْهَقِيُّ فِي « الدَّلَائِلِ » « أَنَّ طَائِفَةً مِنَ الْيَهُودِ حِينَ سَمِعُوا رَسُولَ اللَّهِ ﷺ يَتْلُو هَذِهِ السُّورَةَ) سُورَةَ يوسف (أَسْلَمُوا لِمُوَافَقَتِهَا مَا عِنْدَهُمْ. وَهُوَ مِنْ رِوَايَةِ الْكَلْبِيِّ، عَنْ أَبِي صَالِحٍ، عَنِ ابْنِ عَبَّاسٍ

Ibn Kathir reports in his tafsir that when a faction among the Jews heard the Prophet Muhammad recite this surah (Yusuf), they embraced Islam because its content matched what they had in their scriptures.

This is reported by Al-Bay-haqi in "Ad-Dala'il" and comes from a narration of Al-Kalbi by Abi Salih from Ibn Abbas

---

DUA

PRAY TO ALLAH FOR SUPPORT IN TIMES OF CRISIS

لَا إِلَهَ إِلَّا اللَّهُ الْعَظِيمُ الْحَلِيمُ، لَا إِلَهَ إِلَّا اللَّهُ رَبُّ الْعَرْشِ العَظِيمِ، لَا إِلَهَ إِلَّا اللَّهُ رَبُّ السَّمَوَاتِ ورَبُّ الأَرْضِ ورَبُّ العَرْشِ الكَرِيم

Lā ilāaha illā allaahul-Ad-himul-Halim, lā ilāaha illā allaahu Rabbul-'Ars-hil-'Adhim, lā ilāaha illā allaahu Rabbus-samaa-waati wa Rabbul-'ardhi wa Rabbul-'Arshil-Karim.

Source: Al-Bukhari 8/154, Muslim 4/2092

There is no deity except Allah, the Mighty, the Gentle; there is no deity except Allah, the Lord of the Mighty Throne; there is no deity except Allah, the Lord of the heavens, the Lord of the earth, and the Lord of the Noble Throne.

15

MUSA'S (A.S.) RESCUE FROM PHARAOH

نجاة موسى (ع) من فرعون

MUSA'S (A.S.) RESCUE FROM PHARAOH

At a time when the Pharaoh of Egypt ruled, Musa (a.s.) was born. He was a descendant of the family of Yusuf (a.s.), which had grown over many years and became the people called Bani Israel. This means the Children of Israel, as they were all descended from Yaqûb (a.s.), who was often called Israel.

It was a challenging time for the Bani Israel in Egypt, as a rumor spread throughout the land. Pharaoh had a dream in which it was prophesied that a newborn boy from among the people would rise up and end his reign. Fearing he would lose his throne, Pharaoh ordered all the newborn boys of Bani Israel to be killed.

Musa (a.s.) was born during this terrible time. To save him from this cruel fate, he was first hidden. Then his mother placed him in a small basket and set it on the Nile. Allah (s.w.t.) had spoken to her beforehand and revealed to her that nothing would happen to little Musa (a.s.).

She whispered to Musa (a.s.), "Don't be afraid, my little one. Allah (s.w.t.) will watch over you and take care of you." Miryam, the older sister of Musa (a.s.), watched everything and followed the basket as it floated down the Nile.

As fate would have it, Pharaoh's wife of all people found the basket. She took the little bundle in her arms and immediately felt a deep love for the child. "This boy could bring us luck and blessings," she said to her husband, Pharaoh. "Let's let him grow up like our own son."

But little Musa (a.s.) did not want to be fed by the wet nurses in the palace. Miryam heard about this and bravely stepped forward and said, "I know a woman who can breastfeed the baby."

Pharaoh's wife was relieved and said, "Please, bring her here."

Miryam ran quickly and brought her mother to the palace. The mother was so happy when she held her little Musa (a.s.) in her arms again! She did not show her feelings to protect her son. So, Musa (a.s.) grew up at the Pharaoh's court and was able to stay with his mother at the same time.

When Musa (a.s.) grew up, he became a strong and righteous man. He was brought up like a prince and was educated by the best teachers in Egypt. He realized how unjust the Pharaoh was, especially to the Bani Israel. This displeased Musa (a.s.) greatly.

One day, he saw an Egyptian guard beating an innocent man. "Stop! Why are you doing this?" he shouted indignantly. When the guard did not react, Musa (a.s.) pounced on him, and in the ensuing confrontation, he killed him. Shocked by his deed and fearing punishment for his offense, he fled the city and sought refuge in the desert.

Musa (a.s.) lived in the desert for many years, far away from the splendor of the Egyptian court. He lived a simple life and got to know the hard work of the shepherds. "The desert is not an easy place to live," he sometimes murmured to himself, "but I learned a lot and became stronger as a result."

Musa (a.s.) wandered through the desert until he came to the land of Madyan. It was a hot day and he saw a well where some shepherds were watering their sheep. He also noticed two young girls standing apart because the shepherds would not let them near the well.

Musa (a.s.) went to them and asked kindly, "Why are you waiting here? Do you need help?"

One of the girls replied shyly, "We can't water our sheep because the other shepherds won't let us go to the well. Our father is very old and can't help us."

Musa (a.s.) knew that he could help. He rolled up his sleeves and said resolutely, "Don't worry, I will help you!" With his strength and kindness, Musa (a.s.) helped the girls to water their sheep quickly.

The girls were grateful and rushed home to tell their father about the kind stranger who had helped them. Their father was pleased and asked his daughters to invite Musa (a.s.) so that he could thank him personally. Musa (a.s.) came and told the old man his story. The man was wise and knew that Musa (a.s.) was a good person. He offered him to stay with them and marry one of his daughters.

Musa felt honored and accepted the offer. He found a new home in Madyan and a family who loved him. But Musa (a.s.) knew that he was destined for other tasks, and he was eager to spread his knowledge.

The story of Musa (a.s.) teaches us several important lessons. One of the central lessons is unwavering trust in Allah (s.w.t.). Another lesson is the importance of justice and standing up against oppression, as Musa (a.s.) did when he defended the innocent. The story also emphasizes the importance of modesty, helpfulness, and recognizing divine guidance in our lives.

Sources: The Holy Qur'an:

Sura 20, verses 37-40 | Sura 28, verses 4-28 | Sura 66, verse 11.

HADITH

فقد روي عن أم المؤمنين السيدة عائشة رضي الله عنها أنها قالت: «كانت قريش تصوم عاشوراء في الجاهلية وكان رسول الله - صلى الله عليه وسلم- يصومه فلما هاجر إلى المدينة صامه وأمر بصيامه فلما فرض شهر رمضان قال من شاء صامه ومن شاء تركه»، وأيضاً روي عن الرسول - صلَّى الله عليه وسلَّم- أنه عندما هاجر إلى المدينة المنورّة، وتبيّن له أنَّ اليهود يصومون ذلك اليوم فرحاً بنجاة موسى عليه السلام، قال عليه الصلاة والسلام: أنا أحقُّ بموسَى منكم فصامه رسولُ اللهِ صلَّى الله عليه وسلَّم وأمَرَ بصومِه

It is reported from Aisha (may Allah be pleased with her), the wife of the Prophet, that she said: "The Quraysh fasted on the day of Ashura in the time of pre-Islamic ignorance, and when the Prophet (blessings and peace of Allah be upon him) moved to Medina, he continued to fast on that day and ordered the people to do the same. When the month of Ramadan was prescribed, he said: 'Whoever wishes may fast on the day of Ashura, and whoever does not wish to may refrain. It is also narrated from the Prophet that after he moved to Medina when he heard that the Jews were fasting on the day of Ashura to commemorate the salvation of Musa (peace be upon him), he said, "I am closer to Musa than you," then he fasted on that day and ordered the people to fast.

Narrated by Al-Bukhari and Musli

DUA

PRAYER FOR COURAGE AND STRENGTH
BEFORE GIVING A SPEECH

رَبِّ ٱشْرَحْ لِي صَدْرِي وَيَسِّرْ لِيَ أَمْرِي وَٱحْلُلْ عُقْدَةً مِّن لِّسَانِي يَفْقَهُواْ قَوْلِي

Rabbi šraḥ lī ṣadrī wa-yassir lī 'amrī, wa-ḥlul 'uqdatan min lisānī yafqahū qawlī.

My Lord, give me the willing-ness (to do so) and make my task easier and untie the knot of my tongue so that they may understand my speech.

Source: Sura 20:25-28 (ṭāhā)

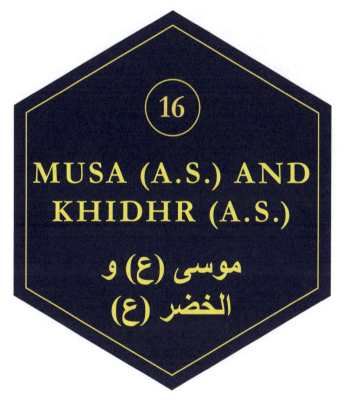

16

MUSA (A.S.) AND KHIDHR (A.S.)

موسى (ع) و
الخضر (ع)

MUSA (A.S.) AND KHIDHR (A.S.)

One day Musa (a.s.) said to the people around him that he had the most knowledge among them. Allah (s.w.t.) heard this and revealed to him that there was someone who had more knowledge. Musa (a.s.) was surprised and curious. He asked Allah (s.w.t.) to allow him to meet this wise man. Allah (s.w.t.) agreed and gave Musa (a.s.) instructions to find this man named Khidhr (a.s.).

Musa (a.s.) and his servant Yusha' bin Nun followed the instructions of Allah (s.w.t.) and set out. They took a fish with them to eat when they became hungry. Allah (s.w.t.) had told Musa (a.s.) that the place where the fish would disappear was the place where he would find Khidhr (a.s.).

After a long journey, they noticed that the fish magically came to life and jumped into the sea. They had reached the place that Allah (s.w.t.) had told them. There they finally met Khidhr (a.s.).

Musa asked Khidhr (a.s.), "May I follow you to learn from your knowledge?" Khidhr (a.s.) looked at Musa (a.s.) and replied, "I am afraid you will not have the patience to follow me. How could you remain calm and patient when you see things that you do not understand?"

Musa (a.s.) promised to be patient and not to question why Khidhr (a.s.) did the things he did. He became Khidhr's (a.s.) disciple. They then started traveling together. During their journey, three strange things happened.

First, Khidhr (a.s.) came to a ship and made a large hole in it. Musa (a.s.) protested as this would harm the fishermen. But Khidhr (a.s.) reminded Musa (a.s.) of his promise to be patient and not to ask questions.

Then he took Musa (a.s.) to a small village. They were both tired and hungry, but when they asked for something to eat, the villagers refused to feed them. Musa was disappointed, but he remained patient. Then he saw Khidhr (a.s.) rebuilding a wall that had almost collapsed. "But the people here were so rude to us," said Musa (a.s.). "Why are you helping them?"

Khidhr (a.s.) smiled and reminded Musa (a.s.) of his promise again. "Didn't you say that you would be patient and not ask questions?" he asked again.

They traveled on and met a boy. To Musa's great surprise, Khidhr (a.s.) killed the boy. Musa (a.s.) was shocked and could not understand why Khidhr (a.s.) had done such a thing. "This is too much!" exclaimed Musa (a.s.) in horror. "You have killed an innocent boy!"

Khidhr (a.s.) only sighed and explained that it was now time to part. After all, Musa (a.s.) had broken his promise three times. Before they parted, Khidhr (a.s.) explained the reasons for his seemingly strange behavior.

The ship he had punched a hole in belonged to poor fishermen. The soldiers of an evil king were on their way to steal it to wage war against innocent people, but because it was now sunk, the fishermen were able to salvage it, repair it, and keep it. Khidhr (a.s.) continued and explained that the wall he had repaired hid a treasure that belonged to two orphans. If the wall had collapsed, the villagers would have discovered the treasure and stolen it. Now that the wall was up, the treasure was safe until the children were old enough to find it. And the boy he had killed would have committed very evil deeds in the future and made his pious parents very unhappy. Allah (s.w.t.) would give them a better son instead.

Musa (a.s.) now understood that not everything that seems bad is really bad. Sometimes things happen for reasons we cannot understand because Allah (s.w.t.) has a better plan.

This story teaches us that we often see things that we do not understand. But Allah (s.w.t.) has a plan, and even if we do not understand it, we should trust that He wants the best for us.

Sources: The Holy Qur'an:

Sura 18, verses 60-82.

HADITH

والخضر سمي بهذا الاسم بالخضر: فتح الخاء، وكسر الضاد؛ لأنه كما
ورد في الحديث الصحيح: أنه جلس على فروة بيضاء، فإذا هي تهتز من
خلفه خضراء

Khidhr was named after the color green (Al-Khadr): This is because it is mentioned in an authentic hadith that he sat on an area without grass, and it turned green when he walked.

Reported by Al-Bukhari: 3402

DUA

PRAYER FOR SUCCESS IN EXAMS

رَّبِّ أَدْخِلْنِي مُدْخَلَ صِدْقٍ وَأَخْرِجْنِي مُخْرَجَ صِدْقٍ وَٱجْعَل لِّي مِن لَّدُنكَ
سُلْطَٰنًا نَّصِيرًا

Rabbi 'adḫilnī mudḫala ṣiduq wa-'aḫriǧnī muḫraǧa ṣiduq wa-ǧ'al lī min ladunka sulṭānan naṣīran.

O my Lord, let my entrance be a good entrance, and let my exit be a good exit. And grant me your helpful strength.

Source: Sura 17:80 (al-'isrā')

17

MUSA (A.S.) LEADS THE CHILDREN OF ISRAEL OUT OF EGYPT

موسى (ع) يخرج بني إسرائيل من مصر

MUSA (A.S.) LEADS THE CHILDREN OF ISRAEL OUT OF EGYPT

Musa (a.s.) and his family were traveling a lot through the desert. It was during a rest when Musa (a.s.) suddenly saw a fire. As he came closer, a voice spoke to him from the fire.

Allah (s.w.t.) said, "O Musa (a.s.)! I am your Lord. Take off your shoes, for you are in the sacred valley of Tuwa. I have chosen you, so listen to what is revealed. I am Allah (s.w.t.), there is no god but me. Worship me and no one else."

Allah (s.w.t.) told Musa (a.s.) about his mission to free the people of the Children of Israel from slavery in Egypt. He said to Musa (a.s.), "Musa (a.s.), I have chosen you. Go back to Egypt and lead my people, the Bani Israel, out of slavery. Go to Pharaoh and tell him to release them but be gentle with him and speak kind words."

Before Musa (a.s.) set out to fulfill his mission, Allah (s.w.t.) wanted to show him something special. Allah (s.w.t.) asked him, "What is that in your right hand?" Musa (a.s.) replied, "This is my stick that I use to support myself, with which I beat the leaves from the bushes for my flocks, and I also use it for other practical things."

Then Allah (s.w.t.) commanded, "Throw it on the ground, Musa (a.s.)!" When Musa (a.s.) threw his stick on the ground, something amazing happened, the stick turned into a writhing snake! Musa (a.s.) was surprised and a little frightened, and he began to take a few steps back. But Allah (s.w.t.) calmed him down and said, "Come closer and do not be afraid." Allah (s.w.t.) then told Musa (a.s.) to take hold of the snake. When Musa (a.s.) did so, the snake turned back into a stick!

Then He said to Musa (a.s.), "Now put your hand in your pocket." Musa (a.s.) did as he was commanded, and when he pulled out his hand, it shone bright white, as if it were made of light! Allah (s.w.t.) told Musa (a.s.) that this was another sign that he should show to Pharaoh. He told Musa (a.s.), "Go to Pharaoh and show him these two signs, but be patient and courageous, because Pharaoh will be stubborn and will not let the Bani Israel go easily."

Musa (a.s.) asked Allah (s.w.t.) to let his brother Harûn (a.s.) help him. Allah (s.w.t.) granted his request and the brothers, who had not seen each other for a long time, were reunited. They set off for Egypt, but on the way to Pharaoh's palace, they began to have some doubts about their mission. They wondered whether Pharaoh would listen to them and whether they would be able to free the children of Israel.

At that moment, Allah (s.w.t.) spoke to them again and gave them courage. He said: "Fear not! I am with you; I hear and see everything. Show Pharaoh the signs and remind him of the miracles I have performed. Be strong and have faith."

Musa (a.s.) and Harûn (a.s.) finally entered the Pharaoh's magnificent palace. They saw him sitting on his golden throne, surrounded by his advisors, who were dressed in fine garments, and eyed them suspiciously.

Musa (a.s.) gathered all his courage and said, "O great Pharaoh, I am Musa (a.s.) and this is my brother Harûn (a.s.). We are messengers from Allah (s.w.t.), the Almighty. He has sent us to convey His words to you and to ask you to release the Children of Israel." Pharaoh just laughed and replied, "Who is this Allah (s.w.t.) you speak of? I am Pharaoh, the ruler of Egypt and the Nile! I have all the power, and that is why I exercise it! Without me, the people of Egypt would have no water and could not farm." Musa (a.s.) replied gently, "Allah (s.w.t.) is the Creator of the universe, the Lord of the worlds. And He has given us signs to prove His power to you."

Pharaoh called out challengingly, "Show me these signs, if they are so wonderful!"

Musa (a.s.) held up his staff and threw it on the ground. Suddenly the staff turned into a huge snake! Everyone in the hall was astonished. Then Musa (a.s.) put his hand inside his shirt, and when he pulled it out again, it shone as brightly as the sun. Everyone was speechless at this miracle.

Pharaoh, trying to keep his composure, said, "This is nothing but magic! I also have magicians who can perform such tricks!" Musa (a.s.) replied, "This is not magic, Pharaoh. These are signs from Allah (s.w.t.). Please let the Children of Israel go so that they can live in peace."

However, Pharaoh did not even think about it but had his best magicians summoned. He wanted to expose Musa (a.s.) in a contest. Pharaoh's magicians stepped forward and bowed. They threw their staffs on the ground and their magic seemed to transform them into snakes. The spectators were impressed, but Musa (a.s.) remained calm. Then he threw his staff on the ground, and to everyone's amazement, he turned into an even bigger snake that devoured all the others!

The magicians immediately fell to their knees and exclaimed, "We believe in the god of Musa (a.s.) and Harûn (a.s.)! He is the true God!"

Pharaoh was furious and furious when he heard this and saw that his magicians were bowing down to Musa (a.s.) and Harûn (a.s.) and accepting faith in Allah (s.w.t.). He called out to them, "How dare you believe in his god without my permission! I will punish you! I will chop off your hands and feet and hang you on palm trees. You will see how powerful I am!"

However, the magicians no longer feared Pharaoh. They replied boldly, "Can you punish us worse than by death? We have seen the truth, and nothing can dissuade us. Judge as you wish to judge. It is up to Allah (s.w.t.), our Lord, to judge us. We hope for His forgiveness, for we are the first to believe in Him."

Pharaoh called Musa (a.s.) into a private room in the palace and addressed him with feigned friendliness, "Musa (a.s.), we have raised you here in the palace. Do you not see all that I have given you? And yet you betray me and oppose me with this new god of yours. I am the Lord of Egypt, and there is no god but me!"

Musa (a.s.) replied calmly, "O Pharaoh, I am not ungrateful for what I have received here, but I serve the true God, the Lord of the Worlds, the Creator of all things. He has shown me that I must bring the truth to the people. You have also treated my people badly and would have had me killed if your wife had not protected me."

Pharaoh replied mockingly, "And what about the generations before us? What will become of them if your God is the only true God?" Musa (a.s.) replied, "The knowledge of them is with my Lord, in a book. My Lord makes no mistakes and forgets nothing."

Pharaoh still did not want to let the Bani Israel go, even after several requests by Musa (a.s.). The borders were more strictly guarded, and escape had become increasingly difficult and dangerous.

So, Allah (s.w.t.) sent ten plagues to Egypt to punish Pharaoh.

First, He turned the water of the Nile into blood. The people could no longer drink from the Nile or cultivate their fields. Musa (a.s.) said to Pharaoh, "Let my people go, or it will get worse!" But Pharaoh persisted.

Soon after, countless frogs were released in Egypt, literally flooding the country. They were everywhere - in the houses, on the streets, in the beds. Pharaoh called Musa (a.s.) to him and said, "Ask your god to make the frogs disappear and I will let your people go." However, when the frogs disappeared, Pharaoh broke his promise.

This was followed by a plague of mosquitoes and sandflies, which tormented people and animals and almost drove them mad. After that, Allah (s.w.t.) sent a plague of wild animals that caused unrest and destruction. The next plague was a disease that struck the livestock and killed most of them. This was followed by another plague of painful boils that affected humans and animals. Finally, the seventh plague consisted of violent hailstorms. After the hail came a plague of locusts that ate everything the hailstorms had left behind. Then came a deep darkness that covered the land for three days and nights. After each plague, Pharaoh asked Musa (a.s.) to ask Allah (s.w.t.) to end the plague, promising each time to release the Bani Israel, only to go back on his word once the plague was over.

Finally, when the tenth and worst plague - the death of all the first-born of Egyptian families - came upon the land, Pharaoh relented and allowed the Bani Israel to leave Egypt. The Children of Israel packed their belongings and set off through the desert in the dark of night. Musa (a.s.) led his people.

No sooner had they left Egypt than Pharaoh regretted his decision and sent his army to bring back the Bani Israel. So, the soldiers, led by Pharaoh, set off in pursuit.

When Musa (a.s.) and the Bani Israel reached the Red Sea, they saw the army approaching and became very afraid. After all, they were trapped and had no ships on which they could flee from the soldiers, but Musa (a.s.) calmed them down and said, "No, indeed, Allah (s.w.t.) is with me. He will guide me rightly." Then he struck the water with his staff and the sea parted so that the people could walk past the floods and pass through dry land.

When they reached the other shore and Pharaoh's army wanted to take the same route, Allah (s.w.t.) caused the sea to collapse again and Pharaoh and his army were swallowed up by the waters. When Pharaoh saw that he was doomed and that the waves of the Red Sea were crashing over him, he cried out in despair that he now believed in the God in whom the children of Israel believed. However, it was too late for Pharaoh, as it was only in the face of death and despair that he acknowledged what he had previously denied. His confession of faith was not considered sincere and came too late to be of any use to him.

Now Musa (a.s.) and the Bani Israel were finally free. They were liberated from the oppression and the heavy burdens they had carried in Egypt. Freedom was a feeling that many of them had never known before. They rejoiced and thanked Allah (s.w.t.) for their salvation.

The story of Musa (a.s.) teaches us humility and patience as well as courage and standing up for justice for the oppressed: Musa (a.s.) courageously stood up against Pharaoh and stood up for the freedom of Bani Israel. The consequences of unbelief and arrogance are also illustrated. Despite numerous signs and miracles, Pharaoh refused to acknowledge Allah (s.w.t.) and ultimately had to bear the consequences of his actions.

Sources: The Holy Qur'an:

Sura 2, verses 46-60 | Sura 7, verses 103-137 | Sura 10, verses 75-93 | Sura 11, verses 96-99 | Sura 17, verses 101-102 | Sura 20, verses 9-79 | Sura 25, verses 35-36 | Sura 26, verses 10-69 | Sura 28, verses 29-46 | Sura 51, verses 38-40.

HADITH

در» مع أنه لم يحتم عليهم: يا رسول الله، لو خضت بنا هذا البحر لخضناه معك، ولو بلغت بنا برك الغماد ما تخلف عنك أحد

ولا نقول كما قال قوم موسى لموسى: { اذْهَبْ أَنتَ وَرَبُّكَ فَقَاتِلَا إِنَّا هَاهُنَا قَاعِدُونَ } ولكن اذهب أنت وربك فقاتلا إنا معكما مقاتلون، من بين يديك ومن خلفك، وعن يمينك وعن يسارك

The Companions said to the Prophet Muhammad when he asked them about participating in the battle on the day of the Battle of Badr, although they were not obliged to do so: "O Messenger of Allah, if you lead us across this sea, we will cross it with you. And if you lead us to the mountains of Ghamad, no one will lag behind you." They did not say, as the people of Musa said to Musa, "You and your master go and fight, we will sit here," but they said, "You and your master go and fight, we are here to fight with you, in front of you, behind you, on your right and your left."

Tafsir Al-Saadi

DUA

PRAYER WHEN YOU LEAVE A CITY

رَبَّنَآ أَخْرِجْنَا مِنْ هَٰذِهِ ٱلْقَرْيَةِ ٱلظَّالِمِ أَهْلُهَا وَٱجْعَل لَّنَا مِن لَّدُنكَ وَلِيًّا وَٱجْعَل لَّنَا مِن لَّدُنكَ نَصِيرًا

Rabbanā ʾaḥriǧnā min hāḏihi l-qaryati ẓ- ẓālimi ʾahluhā wa-ǧʿal lanā min ladunka waliyyan wa-ǧʿal lanā min ladunka naṣīran-i.

O Allah, lead us out of this city whose inhabitants do wrong and give us from You a protector and give us from You a savior.

Source: Sura 4:75 (an-nisāʾ)

18

MUSA (A.S.) BRINGS GOD'S COMMANDMENTS TO THE CHILDREN OF ISRAEL

موسى (ع) يأتي بوصايا الله إلى بني إسرائيل

MUSA (A.S.) BRINGS GOD'S COMMANDMENTS
TO THE CHILDREN OF ISRAEL

After Musa (a.s.) and the Bani Israel left Egypt, they traveled through the desert. Musa (a.s.) led the 12 tribes of the Children of Israel. Many of them were grateful that they had been freed from slavery, but they did not fully trust Musa (a.s.) and Allah (s.w.t.). They were worried about their survival in the desert and complained of hunger and thirst.

Then Musa (a.s.) again asked Allah (s.w.t.) for help. And He said, "Musa (a.s.), strike this rock with your stick." And do you know what happened when Musa (a.s.) struck the rock with his stick? Suddenly, 12 springs gushed forth - one for each of the 12 tribes of Bani Israel! At last, they had found the water they so desperately needed.

And Allah (s.w.t.) had also provided something to eat. They found strange food on the desert floor. They called it "Mannah". Allah (s.w.t.) had given them this food so that they would not go hungry. Some of the Bani Israel began to complain. They said, "Always eating the same thing! In Egypt we had onions, garlic, and sometimes even fish. Here we only have this Mannah!" Musa (a.s.) replied, "O my people, why are you not grateful for what Allah (s.w.t.) has given us? He saved us from Pharaoh and you from slavery; he gave us water and nourished us with Mannah. We should be grateful and have faith in Allah (s.w.t.)."

Nevertheless, many followed Musa (a.s.) only because they did not know the way through the desert. After a while, they came across another people. They worshipped statues and figures that they considered to be their gods. This was strange for the Bani Israel, but some of them were interested in the idols.

One of the children of Israel called out to Musa (a.s.), "Musa (a.s.), look! They have gods they can see and touch. Can't we also have such gods?" Musa (a.s.) and replied, "O my people! You are ignorant. These are not real gods! They are just idols made by humans. They cannot speak, hear, or even help. There is only one true God, Allah (s.w.t.), who created us and freed us from slavery. "Be patient and trust in Allah (s.w.t.). He is the only one who can truly protect and guide us."

Finally, Musa (a.s.) and the Bani Israel reached Mount Sinai.

Then Allah (s.w.t.) spoke to Musa (a.s.) and said, "Musa (a.s.), I want you to climb Mount Sinai. I have something very important that I want to give you and the children of Israel."

Musa (a.s.) was excited and said to his people, "I will go up the mountain to receive a message from Allah (s.w.t.). Please wait here patiently for my return." When Musa (a.s.) climbed the mountain, he felt a wonderful radiance surround him. Then he heard Allah's (s.w.t.) voice, "Musa (a.s.), I give you laws and commandments for the Children of Israel to follow. These commandments will help them to lead a good and righteous life."

Allah (s.w.t.) sent two tablets of stone on which the commandments were written. These were special rules such as "Thou shalt not steal", "Thou shalt honor thy parents", „Thou shalt worship only one God" and others.

Musa (a.s.) asked Allah (s.w.t.), "O Allah (s.w.t.), I want to see You! Can You show Yourself to me?" Allah (s.w.t.) explained to Musa (a.s.) that he could not see Him because no one could see God directly. But to show Musa (a.s.) how powerful He is, He struck a nearby mountain with lightning and the mountain broke into a thousand pieces. Musa (a.s.) fainted due to the tremendous power he had just experienced. When he regained consciousness, he said with great devotion, "O Allah (s.w.t.), I am ever grateful to You and will always worship You."

While Musa (a.s.) was talking to Allah (s.w.t.), strange things happened at the foot of the mountain. The Bani Israel waited and waited, but Musa (a.s.) stayed away for a long time - he spent a total of 40 days and nights on Mount Sinai. Some of the Bani Israel became impatient and began to forget why they were even here. One of the men then suggested that they build a statue of gold that they could worship, just like the people they had seen before. Many agreed and brought their gold together. They melted it down, built a statue in the shape of a calf, and began to worship it.

Harûn (a.s.), the brother of Musa (a.s.), saw this with great concern. He said to them, "My brothers and sisters, you should not do this! Musa (a.s.) taught us to worship only Allah (s.w.t.) and we should wait patiently for him!" But some of them did not listen to Harûn (a.s.) and continued to worship the golden cow.

When Musa (a.s.) came down from the mountain and saw the Bani Israel dancing around the golden calf, he was so enraged that he dropped the tablets. His face turned red with anger, and he shouted in a loud voice, "O my people! How can you do such a thing? Allah (s.w.t.) has delivered us and given us so many signs, and now you are worshipping a golden calf? Have you forgotten the true faith so quickly?"

Then he went to Harûn (a.s.), grabbed him by the beard and head, and shook him. "Why didn't you stop them?" shouted Musa (a.s.). Harûn (a.s.) replied, "Brother, I tried, but they wouldn't listen. I was afraid they might turn against me and even kill me."

Musa (a.s.) found out that a man named Samiri was responsible for the idol worship. When he confronted him, Samiri replied, "I have seen what no one else has seen. We only wanted to worship the calf until you returned." Musa (a.s.) realized that Samiri was lying, deliberately causing trouble, and leading people astray from the right path. He said to him, "Go! You will have to endure a punishment that cannot be avoided. Look at your idol, to which you were devoted. We will burn it and then throw it into the sea!"

So Samiri was punished for his deeds, and the golden calf was burned, and the remains were thrown into the sea.

Musa (a.s.) then gathered the tablets again and called the Bani Israel together. "My people," cried Musa (a.s.), "you have wronged yourselves by worshipping the calf. Now return to your Creator in repentance and kill among yourselves the one who is responsible for what has happened. This will be better for you in the eyes of your Creator. Then turn to Him in repentance. He is the merciful one."

Musa (a.s.) read the commandments to his people and instructed them to always behave according to them.

Some of the Bani Israel felt deep remorse for what they had done. They built an ark made of acacia wood and gold to safely transport the tablets with the commandments; but not all of them were repentant.

From the story of Musa (a.s.) and the Children of Israel, we can learn many valuable lessons, such as the importance of leadership. Musa was a leader who guided his people and encouraged them to do the right thing. However, history also shows the dangers of idolatry and how easily people can be led astray if they are not vigilant.

Sources: The Holy Qur'an:

Sura 2, verses 51-62 | Sura 5, verses 57-48 | Sura 7, verses 138-156 | Sura 20, verses 80-98 | Sura 51, verse 5.

HADITH

وكذلك شأن التشريع أن يلقى إلى الأمة تدريجا كما في حديث عائشة في صحيح البخاري أنها قالت : إنما أنزل أول ما أنزل منه (أي القرآن) سورة من المفصل فيها ذكر الجنة والنار حتى إذا ثاب الناس إلى الإسلام نزل الحلال والحرام ، ولو أنزل أول شيء : لا تشربوا الخمر ، لقالوا : لا نترك الخمر أبدا ، ولو نزل : لا تزنوا : لقالوا : لا ندع الزنى أبدا . لقد نزل بمكة على محمد ـ صلى الله عليه وسلم ـ وإني لجارية ألعب والساعة موعدهم والساعة أدهى وأمر ، وما نزلت سورة البقرة والنساء إلا وأنا عنده

The process of legislation was gradually revealed to the community, as Aisha mentioned in an authentic hadith narrated by Al-Bukhari. She said: "The first verses revealed in the Qur'an were detailed verses about Paradise and Hell. When people were firmly established in Islam, the verses about the permissible and the impermissible were revealed. If the first verses at the beginning had been: 'Do not drink wine', they would have said: 'We will never stop drinking wine'. And if the first verses had been: 'Do not commit adultery', they would have said: 'We will never stop committing adultery'. Verily, these verses were revealed in Mecca when Muhammad was still in Mecca. I was a young girl playing nearby while the Hour (the Day of Judgment) was set as her appointment. The Hour is more terrifying and bitter. The suras Al-Baqara and An-Nisa were revealed while I was present."

Sahih al-Bukhari 4993

DUA

PRAYER FOR SUCCESS IN ALL AREAS

اللَّهُمَّ إِنِّي أَعُوذُ بِكَ مِنْ مُنْكَرَاتِ الْأَخْلَاقِ، وَالْأَعْمَالِ، وَالْأَهْوَاءِ

Allāhumma inni a'ūdhu bika min munkaratil-akhlag, wal-a'mal, wal-ahwa'.

O Allah! I seek refuge in You from undesirable behavior, deeds, and aspirations.

Source: Sunan At-Tirmidhi

19

MUSA (A.S.) AND THE BANI ISRAEL IN THE DESERT

موسى (ع) وبني إسرائيل
في الصحراء

MUSA (A.S.) AND THE BANI ISRAEL IN THE DESERT

After leaving the area around Mount Sinai, Musa (a.s.) and the Bani Israel traveled through the desert. Sometimes it was hard for them because it was so hot and there was not much to eat. They had to learn to trust Allah (s.w.t.) and be patient.

One day, as they were wandering through the desert, they saw a land rich in fruits. Musa (a.s.) said to the Bani Israel, "Allah (s.w.t.) has promised us this wonderful land, but we must be brave and fight for it. We must drive out the idolaters."

Some of the Bani Israel doubted and said, "But the people there are very strong and powerful! We cannot fight against them!" Others replied, "We must trust Allah (s.w.t.). He will stand by us."

Musa (a.s.) encouraged them and said, "Be brave and trust in Allah's (s.w.t.) help! He has guided us through so many difficulties."

But the Bani Israel were afraid and refused to enter the land and fight. They even asked Musa (a.s.) to fight the people alone. Allah (s.w.t.) was not pleased that they did not trust Him and said to Musa (a.s.), "Because they do not believe in My words and are cowards, they will wander in the desert for 40 years before they can enter the land I have promised them."

During this long time in the desert, the Bani Israel had to endure many trials. There were days when they were hungry and thirsty and days when they were afraid. During this time, they also learned that they had to trust in Allah (s.w.t.) and that He was always there to help them.

One day, when the Bani Israel were still wandering in the desert, a man was found in their camp who had been murdered. It was a great mystery, for no one knew who the perpetrator was. The Bani Israel were very worried and asked Musa (a.s.) for advice. They said, "Musa (a.s.), you are our leader, and you talk to Allah (s.w.t.). Please ask Him what we should do."

Musa (a.s.) prayed to Allah (s.w.t.) and Allah (s.w.t.) said to him, "Tell the Bani Israel to sacrifice a cow." Musa (a.s.) went to his people and told them what Allah (s.w.t.) had said, but instead of simply obeying, the Bani Israel began to ask many questions. They asked, "What kind of cow should we sacrifice? Is it a young or an old cow? What color should it be?"

Musa (a.s.) replied, "Allah (s.w.t.) says it should be a cow that is neither too old nor too young and has a beautiful, even color."

The Bani Israel did not stop and kept asking, "But what color exactly? There are so many cows!" Musa (a.s.) replied with slight anger, "Allah (s.w.t.) says it should be a golden yellow cow that is beautiful in the eyes of people." They continued to ask, "What is this cow supposed to have done? Is it supposed to have worked in the field?" Musa (a.s.) said, "Allah (s.w.t.) says it should be a cow that has never worked in the field and is completely free of blemishes."

Finally, the Bani Israel found a cow that met all the requirements and sacrificed it. Then Musa (a.s.) said to them, "Take a bone of the cow and touch the murdered man with it." But before this happened, the culprit revealed himself. The murderer knew that it was useless to lie because Allah (s.w.t.) sees everything. The mistrust among the Bani Israel had thus disappeared.

However, there were still some among them who did not trust Musa (a.s.) and did not pay homage to Allah (s.w.t.). One of them was called Qarûn. He was an extremely rich man. Imagine, he was so rich that the keys to his treasure chambers alone had to be carried by a group of strong men! He had gold, silver, jewels and so many riches that they could hardly be counted, but Qarûn was not happy; he wanted even more. He was proud, conceited, and thought that his wealth made him better than others. He went around bragging about his money and looked down on people who did not have as much as he did. Many were jealous of him. Qarûn even wanted to become a powerful king and rule like the evil Pharaoh once did.

One day, Qarûn decided to throw a big party to show off his wealth and power. He invited many people and dressed himself in the most magnificent robes. He wanted everyone to see how rich and powerful he was. During the feast, as Qarûn stood amidst all his gold and jewels, something incredible suddenly happened. The earth beneath him began to shake and tremble. Then a huge fissure opened up and swallowed Qarûn together with all his treasures!

A man from the crowd said aloud, "If Allah (s.w.t.) had not favored us, He would have let us be swallowed up by the earth. Indeed, the disbelievers will not succeed!" The Bani Israel now realized that it was important to obey Allah (s.w.t.) and do good deeds instead of amassing material wealth.

When Musa (a.s.) and the Bani Israel were back near the promised land, Musa (a.s.) felt that his time in this world was ending. He had fulfilled his mission and gathered the Bani Israel around him and said to them, "My dear people, I will soon be leaving this world, but always remember the teachings that Allah (s.w.t.) has given us. Keep the commandments and be good people. Help each other and be grateful for what you have."

The lessons of history: The Bani Israel were often tested because of their disobedience and lack of trust in Allah (s.w.t.). History teaches us the importance of believing in Allah (s.w.t.) and following His instructions. Gratitude and modesty are also discussed. Through the example of Qarûn, we learn that wealth and pride do not protect us from God's judgment. It is important to be humble and grateful for the blessings we have been given.

Sources: The Holy Qur'an:

Sura 2, verses 67-74 | Sura 5, verses 20-27 | Sura 28, verses 76-82 | Sura 53, verse 36.

HADITH

يروى عن كعب الأحبار أنه قال أصاب الناس قحط شديد على عهد موسى عليه السلام فخرج موسى ببني إسرائيل يستسقي بهم فلم يسقوا حتى خرج ثلاث مرات ولم يسقوا فأوحى الله عز وجل إلى موسى عليه السلام إني لا أستجيب لك ولا لمن معك وفيكم نمام فقال موسى يا رب ومن هو حتى نخرجه من بيننا فأوحى الله عز وجل إليه يا موسى أنهاكم عن النميمة وأكون نماما فقال موسى لبني إسرائيل توبوا إلى ربكم بأجمعكم عن النميمة فتابوا فأرسل الله تعالى عليهم الغيث

This passage also comes from the book "Ihya Ulum al-Din" by Imam al-Ghazali, who is considered one of the greatest scholars of Islam. Due to his significant influence in the preservation and promotion of Islamic sciences, he is often referred to as "Hujjat al-Islam" (The Proof of Islam). The story describes a severe period of drought during the time of the Prophet Musa. Musa sought divine intercession for rain, but God revealed that He would not respond as long as the people remained entangled in slander. Moses informed the people of the need to repent and refrain from slander. After they repented, God sent the rain.

From Imam Al-Ghazali - Ihya
Ulum aD-Din 1/307 3/155

DUA

PRAYER FOR A BLESSED PLACE ON A TRIP

رَّبِّ أَنزِلْنِي مُنزَلًا مُّبَارَكًا وَأَنتَ خَيْرُ ٱلْمُنزِلِينَ

Rabbi 'anzilnī munzalan mubārakan wa-'anta ẖayru l-munzilīna.

My Lord, grant me a blessed shelter; for You are the best, Who provides shelter.

Source:
Sura 23:29
(al-mu'minūn)

 147

20

THE CHILDREN OF ISRAEL AND THEIR LAND

بني إسرائيل وبلادهم

THE CHILDREN OF ISRAEL AND THEIR LAND

When the Children of Israel finally entered the Promised Land and arrived in what is now Palestine, they were faced with a large city ruled by people who worshipped idols. The Bani Israel wanted to win the city for themselves because Allah (s.w.t.) had instructed them to do so and because it was part of the Promised Land.

Allah (s.w.t.) spoke to them and said, "You must take the city, but do so with kindness and forgiveness. Treat the people there well, even if they believe differently from you. And do not forget to obey My word!"

The children of Israel besieged the city and prepared to enter it, but then something bad happened. Some of the leaders of the Children of Israel forgot Allah's (s.w.t.) words. Instead of showing kindness and forgiveness, they decided to fight the inhabitants of the city and kill many of them. One of the leaders shouted, "We must secure this city! We are the chosen ones!" But he forgot what Allah (s.w.t.) had told them to do - to be merciful and just. And what was worse, they let the idol priests escape along with their idols. The priests ran out of the city, taking their idols with them.

The Children of Israel had indeed conquered the city, but they had not followed Allah's (s.w.t.) instructions.

Allah (s.w.t.) was not happy about this and said, "I have taught you kindness and forgiveness, but you chose differently. Always remember that it is important to follow My words and act justly."

The Bani Israel began to spread out. They built wonderful cities, including the holy city of Jerusalem. It was a glorious time in which they lived in peace and prosperity. On Saturdays, they celebrated the Sabbath and did not work - as Allah (s.w.t.) had instructed them. "Look," said one of the elders, "how Allah (s.w.t.) has blessed us. We must be grateful and follow His teachings."

But as sometimes happens when people possess too much, some of the Bani Israel became complacent. Instead of thanking and serving Allah (s.w.t.), they began to neglect their faith. Pleasure and wealth became more important to many than following Allah's (s.w.t.) teachings.

"Who needs prayers when we have so much?" said one of them, laughing.

One day, a strange thing happened in a fishing village. The fish seemed to know that the fishermen were not allowed to fish on the Sabbath, so they came to the surface in droves, right in front of the fishermen. You could see the fish swimming around happily and splashing their fins in the water.

A fisherman exclaimed, "Look at that! So many fish! It would be a shame if we didn't catch them." Another fisherman reminded him, "But today is the Sabbath. Allah (s.w.t.) has told us not to fish today. He gives us six days to work, today we should thank Him and pray."

But the majority did not listen to the wise fisherman and started fishing anyway. But Allah (s.w.t.) saw what they were doing and was not pleased with their disobedience.

He said to them, "Because of your deeds, I will turn you into monkeys so that you will realize how important it is to follow My instructions." And so it happened that those who had broken the law were turned into monkeys.

Nevertheless, the Bani Israel increasingly forgot how important it is to be grateful and to always have Allah (s.w.t.) in their hearts. They felt powerful and thought that they were better than other peoples. One day, however, disaster struck the land again. Other tribes and kingdoms turned against the Bani Israel. These enemies began to attack the towns and villages of Bani Israel. The elders came together and said anxiously, "We must do something! Our people are under attack, and we have no strong leadership." The attackers even stole the tablets with the commandments that Allah (s.w.t.) had once given to Musa (a.s.).

One of the elders suggested, "We need a king to lead and unite us so that we can fight together against our enemies." The Bani Israel turned to a prophet whom they held in high esteem and said to him, "Please, ask Allah (s.w.t.) to send us a king whom we can follow."

The Prophet prayed to Allah (s.w.t.) and Allah (s.w.t.) answered him: "I have chosen a man named Talût as king for the Bani Israel." But when the Bani Israel heard about this, some of them were not satisfied. They said, "Why should he be our king? He is not rich and not of noble lineage!" They were envious, power-hungry, and wanted to be king themselves, but the Prophet explained to them, "Allah (s.w.t.) has chosen him because he is strong in body and faith. That is what makes a true leader." He also promised that the Ark with the tablets would return to the Bani Israel as a sign for all believers.

When King Talût was ready to go into battle with his army, there was a special test that Allah (s.w.t.) had planned for the soldiers. It was a test of obedience and trust in Allah (s.w.t.). The king led his army to a river and said, "Allah (s.w.t.) will test you today by this river. Whoever drinks from it does not belong to me, unless he draws only a handful of water."

Can you imagine how hard that was for the soldiers? They were thirsty and the river looked so refreshing! But Talût told them that they were only allowed to drink a little.

Many of the soldiers could not resist the temptation and drank as much as they could. But some who were strong in faith held back and only took a handful of water. King Talût saw who was obedient and who was not. He said to those who had only drunk a handful, "Only we who have controlled ourselves will go to battle. Allah (s.w.t.) will strengthen us because we have obeyed Him." He sent back the disobedient soldiers and with the others, he went into battle against enemies led by a man called Jalût.

The story contains several important teachings, such as obedience to Allah's (s.w.t.) instructions. The Children of Israel were repeatedly punished for disobeying God's commands. History also emphasizes the importance of humility and gratitude towards the blessings that Allah (s.w.t.) grants. Arrogance and complacency can quickly lead to a fall.

Sources: The Holy Qur'an:

Sura 2, verses 58-59 | Sura 5, verses 47-48 | Sura 2, verses 147-149.

HADITH

قال رسول الله صلى الله عليه وسلم: إِنَّ بَنِي إِسْرَائِيلَ لَمَّا اعْتَدَوْا وَعَلَوْا، وَقَتَلُوا الْأَنْبِيَاءَ، بَعَثَ اللهُ عَلَيْهِمْ مَلِكَ فَارِسَ بُخْتَنَصَّرَ، وَكَانَ اللهُ مَلَّكَهُ سَبْعَ مِئَةِ سَنَةٍ، فَسَارَ إِلَيْهِمْ حَتَّى دَخَلَ بَيْتَ الْمَقْدِسِ فَحَاصَرَهَا وَفَتَحَهَا، وَقَتَلَ عَلَى دَمِ زَكَرِيَّا سَبْعِينَ أَلْفًا، ثُمَّ سَبَى أَهْلَهَا وَبَنِي الْأَنْبِيَاءِ، وَسَلَبَ حُلِيَّ بَيْتِ الْمَقْدِسِ، وَاسْتَخْرَجَ مِنْهَا سَبْعِينَ أَلْفًا وَمِئَةَ أَلْفِ عَجَلَةٍ مِنْ حُلِيٍّ حَتَّى أَوْرَدَهُ بَابِلَ، قَالَ حُذَيْفَةُ: فَقُلْتُ: يَا رَسُولَ اللهِ لَقَدْ كَانَ بَيْتُ الْمَقْدِسِ عَظِيمًا عِنْدَ اللهِ؟ قَالَ: أَجَلْ بَنَاهُ سُلَيْمَانُ بْنُ دَاوُدَ مِنْ ذَهَبٍ وَدُرٍّ وَيَاقُوتٍ وَزَبَرْجَدٍ، وَكَانَ بَلَاطُهُ بَلَاطَةٌ مِنْ ذَهَبٍ وَبَلَاطَةٌ مِنْ فِضَّةٍ، وَعُمُدُهُ مِنْ ذَهَبٍ، أَعْطَاهُ اللهُ ذَلِكَ، وَسَخَّرَ لَهُ الشَّيَاطِينَ يَأْتُونَهُ بِهَذِهِ الْأَشْيَاءِ فِي طَرْفَةِ عَيْنٍ، فَسَارَ بُخْتَنَصَّرُ بِهَذِهِ الْأَشْيَاءِ حَتَّى نَزَلَ بِهَا بَابِلَ، وَأَقَامَ بَنُوا إِسْرَائِيلَ فِي يَدَيْهِ مِئَةَ سَنَةٍ تُعَذِّبُهُمُ الْمَجُوسُ وَأَبْنَاءُ الْمَجُوسِ، فِيهِمُ الْأَنْبِيَاءُ وَأَبْنَاءُ الْأَنْبِيَاءِ، ثُمَّ إِنَّ اللهَ رَحِمَهُمْ، فَأَوْحَى إِلَى مَلِكٍ مِنْ مُلُوكِ فَارِسَ يُقَالُ لَهُ كُورَسُ، وَكَانَ مُؤْمِنًا، أَنْ سِرْ إِلَى بَقَايَا بَنِي إِسْرَائِيلَ حَتَّى تَسْتَنْقِذَهُمْ، فَسَارَ كُورَسُ بِبَنِي إِسْرَائِيلَ وَحُلِيِّ بَيْتِ الْمَقْدِسِ حَتَّى رَدَّهُ إِلَيْهِ، فَأَقَامَ بَنُو إِسْرَائِيلَ مُطِيعِينَ للهِ مِئَةَ سَنَةٍ، ثُمَّ إِنَّهُمْ عَادُوا فِي الْمَعَاصِي، فَسَلَّطَ اللهُ عَلَيْهِمُ ابْطِيانُحُوسَ فَغَزَا بِأَبْنَاءَ مَنْ غَزَا مَعَ بُخْتَنَصَّرَ، فَغَزَا بَنِي إِسْرَائِيلَ حَتَّى أَتَاهُمْ بَيْتَ الْمَقْدِسِ، وَأَحْرَقَ بَيْتَ الْمَقْدِسِ، فَسَبَى أَهْلَهَا، وَقَالَ لَهُمْ: يَا بَنِي إِسْرَائِيلَ إِنْ عُدْتُمْ فِي الْمَعَاصِي عُدْنَا عَلَيْكُمْ بِالسَّبَاءِ، فَعَادُوا فِي الْمَعَاصِي، فَسَيَّرَ اللهُ عَلَيْهِمُ السَّبَاءَ الثَّالِثَ مَلِكَ رُومِيَّةَ، يُقَالُ لَهُ قَاقِسُ بْنُ إِسْبَايُوسَ، فَغَزَاهُمْ فِي الْبَرِّ وَالْبَحْرِ، فَسَبَاهُمْ وَسَبَى حُلِيَّ بَيْتِ الْمَقْدِسِ، وَأَحْرَقَ بَيْتَ الْمَقْدِسِ بِالنِّيرَانِ، فَقَالَ رَسُولُ اللهِ صلى الله عليه وسلم: هَذَا مِنْ صَنْعَةِ حُلِيِّ بَيْتِ الْمَقْدِسِ، وَيَرُدُّهُ الْمَهْدِيُّ إِلَى بَيْتِ الْمَقْدِسِ، وَهُوَ أَلْفُ سَفِينَةٍ وَسَبْعُ مِئَةِ سَفِينَةٍ، يُرْسَى بِهَا عَلَى يَافَا حَتَّى تُثْقَلَ إِلَى بَيْتِ الْمَقْدِسِ، وَبِهَا يَجْمَعُ اللهُ الْأَوَّلِينَ وَالْآخِرِينَ

The Prophet Muhammad (peace be upon him) narrated: "When the Children of Israel wronged, transgressed, and killed the prophets, Allah sent Bukhtanassar, the Persian king, over them. Allah established him as ruler over them for seven hundred years. He marched against them until he reached Jerusalem, besieged it, and conquered it. He killed seventy thousand people, captured the inhabitants and the descendants of the prophets, plundered the jewelry of the temple in Jerusalem, and took a hundred thousand camels with treasures to Babylon. Hudhayfah said, 'O Messenger of Allah, was that not a place honored by Allah?' He replied, 'Yes, Sulaimān son of Davūd built it out of gold, pearls, coral, and hyacinths. The tiles on its floor were made of gold and silver. Allah granted him all this and he subjected the demons to his service and forced them to bring him these things in an instant. Bukhtanassar brought these things to Babylon. Then Allah revealed to a believing Persian king, Khoras, that he should return to save the remnants of the Children of Israel. He marched with them until he brought them back to Jerusalem, where the Children of Israel remained obedient to Allah for a hundred years. Then they relapsed into disobedience and Allah handed them over to the Roman king Anushrovan. He attacked them by land and sea, captured them, took the jewels of the Temple in Jerusalem, and burned down the Temple. The Prophet (peace be upon him) said: 'This is the result of the deeds of the jewels of the Temple of Jerusalem'. The Mahdi will bring them back to Jerusalem. He will have a thousand and seven hundred boats that he will use to bring them to Jaffa. From there he will bring them to Jerusalem. With these ships, Allah will bring together the old and the new."

Al-Suyuti, Al Dhar Almanthur (165/4)

DUA

PRAYER FOR PATIENCE

رَبَّنَآ أَفْرِغْ عَلَيْنَا صَبْرًا وَثَبِّتْ أَقْدَامَنَا وَٱنصُرْنَا عَلَى ٱلْقَوْمِ ٱلْكَفِرِينَ

Rabbanā 'afriġ 'alaynā ṣabran wa-ṯabbit 'aqdāmanā wa-nṣurnā 'alā l-qawmi l-kāfirīna.

Our Lord, grant us abundant patience and strengthen our steps, and help us against the people of the unbelievers.

Source: (al-ba-qarah) 2:250

**"So stand firm. The promise of Allah ﷻ is certain.
And let not those who are not convinced make
you waver."**

(Ar-Rum 30:60)

Please pause for a moment.

Ibrahim Al-Abadi and Islam Way are convinced that we Muslims must always remain united, strengthen and spread Islam together. So if you like this book, please feel free to recommend it to your family, friends and loved ones. Even non-Muslims can use this book to learn about Islam and find the way to Allah ﷻ. If you like this book, please help us by leaving an honest review.

You can review the book by clicking on the following link or scanning the QR code:

[Link: https://www.amazon.co.uk/review/create-review/?ie=UTF8&channel=-glan-%20ce-detail&asin=3989290843]

Did you find any errors? Of course we are open to your criticism and welcome your suggestions so that we can further develop this work to the greater satisfaction of Allah ﷻ.
Do not hesitate to send us an email to **info@islamway-books.com**.

Shukran.

Ibrahim Al-Abadi and Islam Way

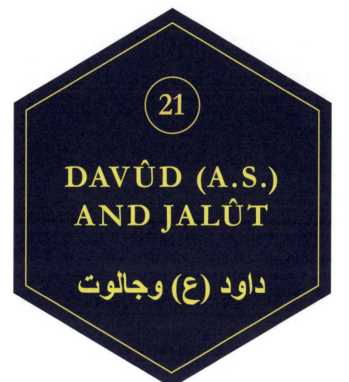

21

DAVÛD (A.S.) AND JALÛT

داود (ع) وجالوت

DAVÛD (A.S.) AND JALÛT

Jalût was not only the leader of the enemies of Bani Israel but a giant of a man.

Under the leadership of their king Talût, they encountered Jalût's army. They were intimidated by Jalût, for he was tall, strong, and seemed invincible. Jalût laughed and shouted, "Who dares to fight me?"

Among the Bani Israel was a young man named Davûd (a.s.). He was still young and not a soldier, but a shepherd grazing his sheep nearby. When he heard Jalût's challenge, he was not intimidated like the others. Instead, he trusted in Allah's (s.w.t.) help and protection and said, "I will fight Jalût."

The soldiers were surprised. "You are just a boy, and he is a mighty warrior," they warned. But Davûd (a.s.) replied, "I trust in Allah (s.w.t.) and He will help me."

King Talût gave Davûd (a.s.) his armor and sword, but Davûd (a.s.) felt uncomfortable in them and instead took his sling and five smooth stones from a nearby stream.

When Davûd (a.s.) stepped onto the battlefield, Jalût laughed and made fun of him, but Davûd (a.s.) was not deterred. He shouted, "With Allah's (s.w.t.) help, I will defeat you!" Then he took one of his stones, put it in his sling, and hurled it with all his might.

The stone hit Jalût right on the temple and the mighty warrior fell to the ground dead. His army fled in fear and terror, they realized that a higher power must have helped Davûd (a.s.).

Davûd (a.s.) was the hero of the day, and later he was crowned king of Bani Israel.

The lesson from this story is that anyone with courage and trust in Allah (s.w.t.) can overcome even the greatest challenges. It is not physical superiority that matters, but devotion to Him.

Sources: The Holy Qur'an:

Sura 2, verse 251.

HADITH

وقد ذكر ابن جرير في « تاريخه » : أن جالوت لما بارز طالوت ،
فقال له : اخرج إلي أو أخرج إليك فندب طالوت الناس ، فانتدب داود ،
فقتل جالوت

Ibn Jarir mentioned in his "Tarikh" that when Jalût fought Talût, he said to him: "Either you come to me, or I will come to you." The people despaired and Talût chose Dawûd to fight Jalût. Dawûd defeated Jalût.

The Beginning and the End:
The Story of Dawûd 2/300

DUA

PRAYER FOR RIGHTEOUSNESS ON THE DAY OF ARAFAH

لاَ إِلَهَ إِلاَّ الله وَحْدَهُ لاَ شَرِيكَ لَهُ لَهُ الْمُلْكُ وَلَهُ الْحَمْدُ وَهُوَ عَلَى كُلِّ شَيْءٍ
قَدِ يرٌ

Lā ilāaha illā allāhu, wahdahu lā sharika lahu lahu l-mulku wa-lahu l-hamdu wa-huwa 'alā kullu shayiin gadirun.

Source: Jami`
at-Tirmidhi
3585

There is no deity except Allah, the One and Only, Who has no partner, His is the dominion and to Him belongs the praise and He has power over all things.

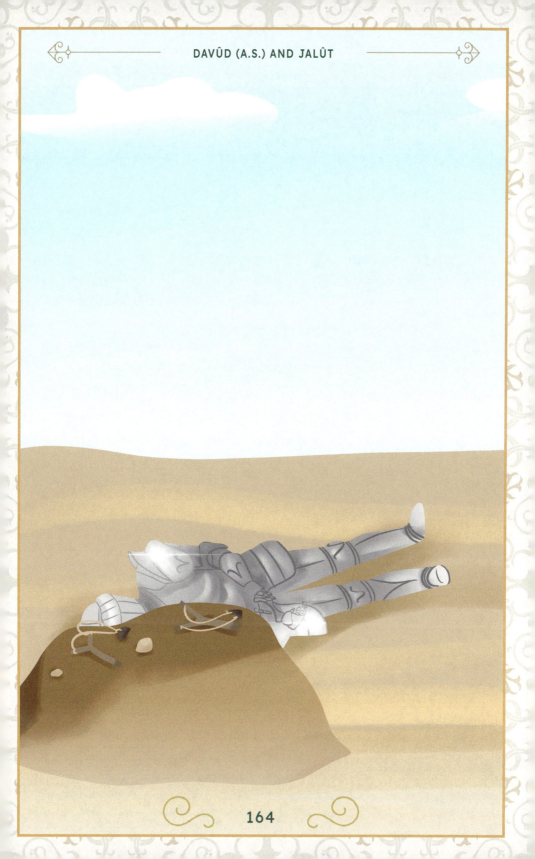

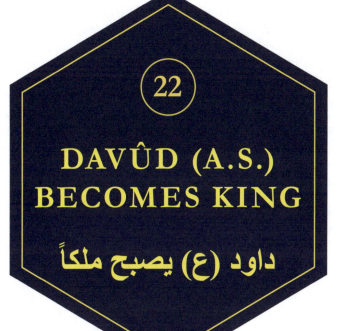

22

DAVÛD (A.S.) BECOMES KING

داود (ع) يصبح ملكاً

DAVÛD (A.S.) BECOMES KING

After Davûd (a.s.) defeated Jalût, people were impressed by his bravery and his trust in Allah (s.w.t.). King Talût invited him to live with him in the palace and he raised him as his son. When King Talûd died one day, Davûd (a.s.) was crowned his successor. The Israelites did not doubt that Davûd (a.s.) had been chosen by Allah (s.w.t.) to be their leader. So Davûd (a.s.) had to lead and protect his people.

He was a just and wise king. He led the people according to the commandments of Allah (s.w.t.) and ensured that justice and fairness prevailed in his kingdom. He treated all people equally, regardless of their rank or origin, and always worked for the welfare of his people.

Davûd (a.s.) had received a special gift from Allah (s.w.t.) - he had a beautiful voice, and when he sang the psalms given to him by Allah (s.w.t.), all living creatures, even the birds, listened and praised Allah (s.w.t.) with him.

Suddenly he saw two men come through a wall into his room! Yes, you read that right, they came through the wall! Davûd (a.s.) was a little frightened, but he knew that Allah (s.w.t.) would help him.

One of the men said, "Do not be afraid, Davûd (a.s.). We are two brothers seeking your advice. My brother here has 99 sheep, while I have only one sheep. He wants me to give him my only sheep, but that doesn't seem fair to me."

Davûd (a.s.) listened attentively and then said in a gentle voice, "It is true that your brother is doing you an injustice by asking for your only sheep while he has so many. He should be more generous." Davûd (a.s.) made them realize that the brother with the 99 sheep was driven by greed and that it is unjust to always want more, especially at the expense of others. He emphasized the importance of being fair and just, and not being driven by greed.

The men nodded and thanked Davûd (a.s.) for his wise advice. Then they disappeared as mysteriously as they had come. Davûd (a.s.) understood that this had been a test from Allah (s.w.t.) and he fell on his knees to pray.

This encounter made Davûd (a.s.) realize that as king and judge, he must always be just and impartial. He was reminded of how easy it is to be tempted by power and wealth and to stray from the right path - like so many kings before him. It was also a warning for Davûd (a.s.) to be critical of his actions and decisions and to ensure that greed or personal interests never influenced him. King Davûd (a.s.) adhered to this throughout his life and ruled the people of Bani Israel justly.

The lesson we learn from the story of King Davûd (a.s.) is the importance of justice and fairness. It does not matter how powerful or rich someone is; what matters is how others are treated and whether the right thing is done. Greed, on the other hand, leads to nothing good.

> **Sources:** The Holy Qur'an:
>
> Sura 38, verses 17-30 | Sura 21, verses 78-82 | Sura 38, verses 17-26.

HADITH

قَالَ رَسُولَ اللَّهِ صلى الله عليه وسلم : أَحَبُّ الصَّلَاةِ إِلَى اللَّهِ صَلَاةُ دَاوُدَ عَلَيْهِ السَّلَامُ ، وَأَحَبُّ الصِّيَامِ إِلَى اللَّهِ صِيَامُ دَاوُدَ ، وَكَانَ يَنَامُ نِصْفَ اللَّيْلِ وَيَقُومُ ثُلُثَهُ وَيَنَامُ سُدُسَهُ ، وَيَصُومُ يَوْمًا وَيُفْطِرُ يَوْمًا

The Prophet Muhammad said: "The prayer most beloved of God is the prayer of Davûd and the fast most beloved of God is the fast of Davûd. He slept half the night, got up for a third, slept for a sixth, and fasted alternately for a day and broke the fast every other day."

Al-Bukhari 1131 and Muslim 1159

DUA

PRAYER FOR THE PROTECTION FROM OUR FELLOW HUMAN BEINGS

اللهم إنا نجعلك في نحورهم، ونعوذ بك من شرورهم

Allāhumma innā naj'aluka fee nuhurihim wa na'ūdhu bika min shururihim.

O Allah, we ask You to restrain them by their necks, and we seek refuge in You from their evil.

Source: Abu Dawud 2/89

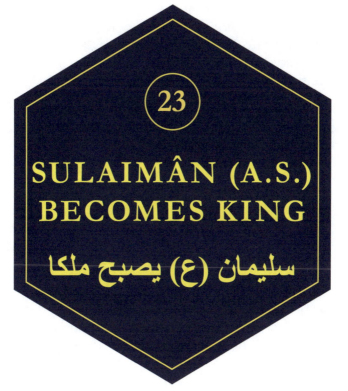

23

SULAIMÂN (A.S.) BECOMES KING

سليمان (ع) يصبح ملكا

SULAIMÂN (A.S.) BECOMES KING

One day, when King Davûd (a.s.) was getting older, he knew that his days were ending. He had many sons, but one of them, Sulaimân (a.s.), was particularly clever and wise, even as a young man. Therefore, Davûd (a.s.) chose Sulaimân (a.s.) as his successor. He said to him, "Sulaimân (a.s.), my son, you have a wise soul and a big heart. I see in you a future king."

The people were happy about this choice because they knew that Sulaimân (a.s.) would be a just and wise leader. Even in his childhood, Sulaimân (a.s.) was known as a righteous person.

Finally, Sulaimân (a.s.) became king after his father Davûd (a.s.) died. He prayed to Allah (s.w.t.) and asked for wisdom and advice to guide his people. He asked the Almighty, "O Allah (s.w.t.), please give me the wisdom and understanding to guide my people well." Allah (s.w.t.) answered his prayer. He gave him wisdom, judgment, and the special ability to talk to animals!

As king, Sulaimân (a.s.) was very modest and generous. Instead of keeping his wealth for himself, he distributed it among the people. He took care of the poor and needy and helped them in every way. Although he was a king, Sulaimân (a.s.) worked hard and even earned his daily bread with his own hands. One day, Sulaimân (a.s.) found a lifeless figure sitting on his throne that looked exactly like him. This was a sign from Allah (s.w.t.) to remind him that life is transient and that he should always behave humbly and thank Him for all the gifts he had been given.

Sulaimân (a.s.) decided to build a magnificent temple called Bayt al-Maqdis so that people could pray and worship Allah (s.w.t.) there. The temple was particularly magnificent. It was built with the help of the jinn who obeyed Sulaimân (a.s.). It was a place of prayer and worship for many years.

Once, when Sula'imân (a.s.) was marching across a plain with his huge army of humans and jinn, he heard a small ant speaking to its fellow ants thanks to the special ability Allah (s.w.t.) had given him. This ant called out to the others, "Go to your homes, otherwise you will be trampled on by Sulaimân (a.s.) and his army without them even realizing it!" But Sulayman heard this and smiled. He was touched by the ant's concern and stopped his army so that no ant would be harmed. This shows how Sula'imân (a.s.) cared for all living creatures, great and small.

The story of King Sulaimân (a.s.) teaches us that true wisdom and power come from Allah (s.w.t.). It teaches us to be humble and to use our gifts and abilities for the benefit of others. And it reminds us that we should always thank Allah (s.w.t.) for what He gives us.

Sources: The Holy Qur'an:

Sura 21, verses 78-82 | Sura 38, verses 30-40 | Sura 27, verses 15-19.

HADITH

قال الله تبارك وتعالى عن نبيه سليمان: {وَوَرِثَ سُلَيْمَانُ دَاوُودَ وَقَالَ يَا أَيُّهَا النَّاسُ عُلِّمْنَا مَنطِقَ الطَّيْرِ} [النمل: ١٦]، الوارث هو نبي الله سليمان، والموروث هو أبوه نبي الله داود، وهذا الميراث ليس ميراث مال، وإنما هو ميراث الحكمة، ميراث النبوة، ميراث العلم، بدليل أنه قد عُلم من كتب السير أن داود عليه الصلاة والسلام كان له من الأولاد كثير، حتى إنه قيل: له تسعة عشر ولداً، فكيف يكون الوارث سليمان وحده، ثم كذلك قد نص النبي الكريم - صلوات الله وسلامه عليه - على أن الأنبياء لا يورثون فقال: «نحن معاشر الأنبياء لا نورث»(١)، وقال: «إن الأنبياء لم يورثوا درهماً ولا ديناراً»(٢)، ثم لو كان الميراث المذكور في السورة من القرآن هو ميراث المال لكان ذكره دون فائدة؛ لأنه معلوم من الضرورة أن الولد يرث أباه، وإنما أراد ميراثاً آخر، ألا وهو ميراث النبوة، والعلم، والحكمة

God, the Blessed and Exalted, said about His Prophet Sulaimân: "And Sulaimân inherited from Davûd. He said, "O people, we have been taught the language of birds." (Surah An-Naml, 27:16). The inheritor is the Prophet of God, Sulaimân, and the inheritor is his father, the Prophet of God, Davûd. This inheritance is not a material inheritance, but it is an inheritance of wisdom, a prophetic inheritance, an inheritance of knowledge. The proof of this is that it is known from the historical writings that Davûd, peace be upon him, had many children, so many that he was said to have had nineteen children. How could Sulaimân alone be the heir in this case? Moreover, the beloved Prophet, peace and blessings of God be upon him, clearly stated that the prophets do not leave any material inheritance, saying, "We, the prophets, do not leave any inheritance" (1), and "The prophets do not leave dirhams or dinars as inheritance" (2). Thus, if the inheritance mentioned in the Qur'an had been a material inheritance, it would not have been mentioned, as it is obvious that children inherit from their parents. Rather, the intention was a different kind of inheritance, namely the inheritance of prophethood, knowledge, and wisdom.

(1) Al-Bukhari (3093) and Muslim (1759)

(2) Abu Dawood (3641), At-Tirmidhi (2682) and Ibn Majah (223)

DUA

PRAYER FOR FORGIVENESS AND MERCY

اللَّهُمَّ إِنِّي أَسْأَلُكَ بِرَحْمَتِكَ الَّتِي وَسِعَتْ كُلَّ شَيْءٍ أَنْ تَغْفِرَ لِي

Allāhumma 'inni 'as'aluka birahmatikal-lati wasi'at kulla shay'in 'an taghfira li.

O Allah, I ask You by Your mercy, which encompasses everything, to forgive me.

Source: Ibn Madscha 1753

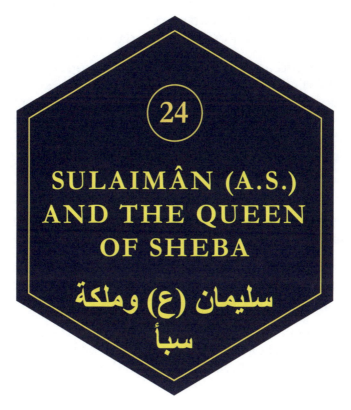

24

SULAIMÂN (A.S.) AND THE QUEEN OF SHEBA

سليمان (ع) وملكة سبأ

SULAIMÂN (A.S.) AND THE QUEEN OF SHEBA

King Sulaimân (a.s.) ruled wisely over his kingdom. One day he noticed that one of his bird messengers was missing. When he returned, he told Sulaimân (a.s.) about a distant land called Saba.

The bird hopped up and down happily and reported excitedly, "O King Sulaimân (a.s.)! I have discovered the wonderful land of Sheba! It is ruled by a queen who has a magnificent throne, but the strange thing is that she and her people worship the sun instead of Allah (s.w.t.)!" Sulaimân (a.s.) frowned and said, "That is not right, Allah (s.w.t.) is the only one we should worship! He created us all and provides for us every day."

The bird nodded eagerly and added, "Yes, King Sulaimân (a.s.), and they also live in great wealth, but they do not know how important it is to worship Allah (s.w.t.) and thank Him for it!"

So Sulaimân (a.s.) decided to send a letter to the Queen of Sheba inviting her to choose the right path and worship Allah (s.w.t.). He sealed the letter and gave it to the bird to take it to Sheba.

When the Queen of Sheba received the letter, she did not know what to do. She was surprised that she had received a letter from such a distant land without having seen the messenger. She read the letter, "In the name of Allah (s.w.t.), the Merciful, the Compassionate. Do not rise up against me but come to me in submission and turn to Allah (s.w.t.)." These lines worried the queen.

So, she called her advisors, including the priests and scholars, to her and asked, "I have received a letter from King Sulaimân (a.s.). He asks us to worship Allah (s.w.t.) and not the sun. What should we do now?"

The priests trembled with fear because they thought that if the queen listened to Sulaimân (a.s.), they would lose all their power. They claimed that they were sons of the sun and told the people that they had special powers. But they only wanted to use their power and control people. One of them, with a long beard and a high-pitched voice, exclaimed, "O Queen, we are mighty sons of the sun! We must not bow down to this king! We must declare war on him!"

The queen was wise and thoughtful. She said, "War brings much suffering and destruction. I will send gifts to King Sulaimân (a.s.) and see how he reacts."

The priests were not happy about it, but the queen had spoken.

When the gifts reached Sulaimân (a.s.), the king was not impressed. With a smile on his face, he said, "Do you want to impress me with wealth? But what Allah (s.w.t.) has given me is more valuable than anything you possess! Keep your gifts, they will not make me rich."

King Sulaimân (a.s.) returned the gift and sent word to the queen that she should surrender to him.

When the queen learned of Sulaimân's (a.s.) reply, she set out to travel to him personally. Sulaimân (a.s.) prepared for her visit.

King Sulaimân (a.s.) wanted to impress the Queen of Sheba and show her the power and gifts that Allah (s.w.t.) had bestowed upon him. He asked his powerful servants which of them would be able to bring the queen's magnificent throne to him before she arrived at his palace.

A strong jinn agreed to bring the throne in a moment. He said to Sulaimân (a.s.), "I will bring it to you before you get up from your seat. I am certainly strong and trustworthy enough to do so." Like lightning, the jinn fetched the queen's throne and brought it to King Sulaimân (a.s.). He arranged for the throne to be altered in a certain way. Sulaimân (a.s.) wanted to test it and see whether the queen would be clever enough to recognize her throne. She would only be able to do this if she was free from selfishness.

When the queen was then received by Sulaimân (a.s.), she was asked whether the throne she saw before her resembled her throne. She recognized the throne and was astonished at what she saw. She did not understand how this was possible.

After the Queen of Sheba recognized the throne, King Sulaimân (a.s.) led her to his magnificent palace. He said to her, "Please enter the palace."

When the queen entered the palace, she carefully lifted her dress, thinking she was wading through water. Then she realized that the floor was made of glass, and it only looked like water! Sulaimân (a.s.) explained to her with a smile, "This is a glass floor in my palace." The queen was amazed and astonished at the wisdom, artistry, and wonders that Sulaimân (a.s.) enjoyed by Allah's (s.w.t.) favor.

She realized the true power and mercy of Allah (s.w.t.) and decided to change her faith and accept Him.

She prayed, "My Lord, I have wronged myself, and now I surrender with Sulaimân (a.s.) to Allah (s.w.t.), the Lord of the worlds." After the Queen of Sheba had accepted Allah (s.w.t.) as the only God, she returned to her people and proclaimed the message of monotheism to them. She explained to them that there is only one God whom they should all worship.

The people of Sheba were impressed by the wisdom and courage of their queen. They recognized the truth in her words and began to worship Allah (s.w.t.) alone. They destroyed their idols and built houses of worship where they could worship Allah (s.w.t.).

After Sulaimân's (a.s.) death, however, there were not always kings who were as wise, God-fearing, and just as he was. Over the years, the kingdom became weaker. The successors of King Sulaimân (a.s.) were unable to maintain the unity of the empire and the magnificent temple that he had once built was destroyed.

This story teaches us that true power and wealth come from our devotion to Allah (s.w.t.) and not from worldly goods. We should always worship Allah (s.w.t.) and be grateful to Him, no matter how big or small our gifts are.

Source: The Holy Qur'an:

Sura 27, verses 20-44 | Sura 34, verses 16-22.

HADITH

عن رسول الله ﷺ أنه قال: «خرج نبي من الأنبياء بالناس يستسقون، فإذا هم بنملة رافعة إحدى قوائمها» - على ظهرها ورافعة إحدى قوائمها - وفي رواية: «تستسقي، تدعو الله أن يسقي الأرض، فقال: ارجعوا، فقد كُفيتم بدعاء هذه النملة»، وفي رواية: «ارجعوا فقد سقيتم بدعوة غيركم»(١)، وجاء عن الزهري مرسلاً أن هذا النبي هو سليمان صلوات الله وسلامه عليه، وهذا أخرجه ابن عساكر في «تاريخه» (٢)

The Prophet reported: "A prophet among the prophets went out with his people to ask Allah for rain. When they passed by an ant, one of its legs was lifted up." In another version, he said: "You may return, for you have been satisfied by the supplication of this ant." In another tradition, he said, "Return, for you have been watered by the supplication of another community." (1) According to Al-Zuhri, this Prophet was Sulaimân, may God's blessings and peace be upon him, and this was reported by Ibn Asakir in his "History". (2)

(1) Reported by At-Tahawi in „Mushkil al-Athar" (732)

(2) "History of Damascus" (22/288)

DUA

PRAYER FOR PROTECTION FROM FALSE GODS

اللَّهُمَّ إِنِّي أَعُوذُ بِكَ أَنْ أُشْرِكَ بِكَ وَأَنَا أَعْلَمُ، وَأَسْتَغْفِرُكَ لِمَا أَعْلَمُ

Allāhumma inni a'ūdhu bika an ashrika bika wa-anä a'lamu, wa-astaghfiruka li-mä lä alam.

O Allah, I seek refuge in You, from knowingly committing evil against You, and I ask Your forgiveness for what I do not know.

Source:
al-Adab
al-Mufrad 716
(al- Bukhari)

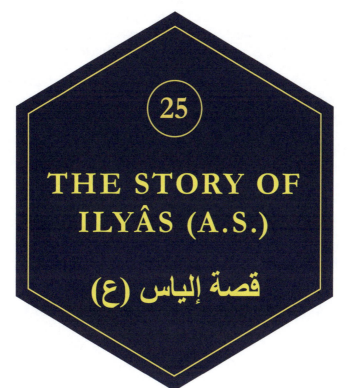

25

THE STORY OF ILYÂS (A.S.)

قصة إلياس (ع)

THE STORY OF ILYÂS (A.S.)

When Sulaimân (a.s.) had been dead for some time, the Bani Israel forgot Allah (s.w.t.). They stopped thanking and worshipping Him and instead began to worship an idol called Baal. It was said that they even sacrificed their children to him.

Allah (s.w.t.), the Almighty, wanted to help the Bani Israel to get back on the right path. That is why He sent Ilyâs (a.s.) to them. Ilyâs (a.s.) was a brave and wise prophet.

He stood before the people and said in a firm voice, "O Bani Israel, why have you forgotten Allah (s.w.t.) who has granted you so many benefits? This idol cannot do you any good. Return to Allah (s.w.t.)!"

The people though, would not listen to him. They made fun of him and continued with their idolatry. Ilyâs (a.s.) was disappointed by this, but he did not give up until he was finally thrown out of the city.

So it happened that despite the urgent warnings of Ilyâs (a.s.) and other righteous people, the Bani Israel continued to worship their idols and turned away from Allah (s.w.t.). Enemy armies conquered Jerusalem, destroyed large parts of the city, and even killed the king.

The survivors below Bani Israel lived in captivity for a long time. For 70 years they were captives who tried to remember Allah (s.w.t.) and His guidance. They had already realized that they had fallen into this difficult situation because they had forgotten Allah (s.w.t.) and worshipped idols instead.

The story of Ilyâs (a.s.) teaches us that faith in Allah (s.w.t.) gives us hope and comfort in challenging times. It reminds us that we should be steadfast in our faith in Allah (s.w.t.) and never stop worshipping Him.

Sources: The Holy Qur'an:

Sura 6, verse 85 | Sura 37, verses 123-132.

HADITH

وأما كلمة ياسين المكتوبة في المصحف بحروفها الخمسة الملفوظة فهي اسم رسول من رسل الله، ويقال له إلياس، وآل ياسين أهل إلياس الذين اتبعوه؛ قال العيني في عمدة القاري (١): قَالَ ابْن عَبَّاس. قَوْله: (وَآل ياسين) ، المُرَاد مِنْهُم الَّذين فِي قَوْله تَعَالَى: وَإِن إِلْيَاس لمن الْمُرسلين

The word "Yasin", as written in the Qur'an with its five pronounced letters, is the name of a messenger among the messengers of God, who is also called Ilyâs. The "Ahl Yasin" refers to the family of Ilyâs and those who followed him. Al-Ayni in "Ummdat al-Qari" said: Ibn Abbas said about the mention of the "Ahl Yasin" in the verse: "They refer to those of whom it says in the verse: 'And certainly, Ilyâs is one of the Messengers.'"

Reported by Al-Ayni in
"Ummdat al-Qari"

DUA

PRAYER FOR SEEKING REFUGE IN ALLAH

اللَّهُمَّ إِنِّي أَعُوذُ بِعِزَّتِكَ لاَ إِلَهَ إِلاَّ أَنْتَ أَنْ تُضِلَّنِي أَنْتَ الْحَيُّ الَّذِي لاَ يَمُوتُ وَالْجِنُّ وَالإِنْسُ يَمُوتُونَ

A'ūdhu bieizatik aladhi lā ilāaha illā 'anta aladhi la yamūtu waljinu wal'iins yamutūna.

I take refuge in Your majesty, in You, besides Whom there is no god, in Him Who does not die, and the jinn and men die.

Source: Sahih
Muslim 2717

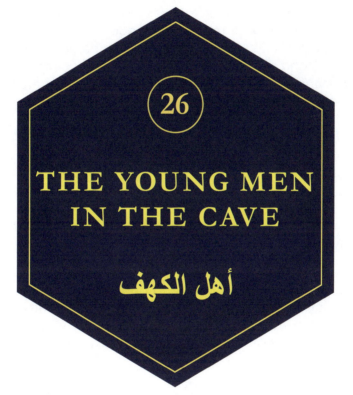

26

THE YOUNG MEN IN THE CAVE

أهل الكهف

THE YOUNG MEN IN THE CAVE

Once upon a time, there was a group of young men who lived in a city where people no longer believed in Allah (s.w.t.). Their tyrannical king had declared himself a god and punished all those who did not worship him. But the young men firmly believed in Allah (s.w.t.) and did not want to take part in idolatry. However, this was dangerous in those days, as the king had his enemies mercilessly persecuted.

So, the young men thought about what they could do.

"We are no longer safe here and do not want to believe in idols," said one of the young men. "We must turn to Allah (s.w.t.) alone and worship Him."

"Yes, you're right," replied another. "Let's find a place where we can pray in peace, away from the idols."

The young men and their dog searched for a secluded place and finally found a cave. They entered and began to pray to Allah (s.w.t.). They asked for forgiveness for their sins for guidance, and protection. Allah (s.w.t.) answered their prayers and put them in a deep sleep that lasted for many, many years in which He protected them.

While they slept, the dog kept watch outside the cave and the world around them changed. The tyrannical king had died a long time ago and the people's situation had improved. When the young men finally woke up, they felt as if they had only slept for a few hours. They were hungry and wanted something to eat. One of the young men said, "I'll go into town and look for something to eat. I'll be careful so that no one discovers us."

So, he took some money they had with them and set off for the city. But do you know what? The town was not the same as it was when they fell asleep in the cave! The buildings looked different, and the people wore strange clothes that the young man had never seen before. When he tried to buy food with the coins, the people were astonished and asked him where he got these old coins. He did not understand what was going on until he realized that a lot of time must have passed, and his coins were no longer accepted as a means of payment! An old man exclaimed, "These coins must be 100 years old!"

So, he returned to his friends in the cave and told them about the changes in the city. They all realized that Allah (s.w.t.) had protected them for many years. "We have truly witnessed a miracle," said one of the youths. "Allah (s.w.t.) protected us while we were sleeping." "Yes, we must be grateful for these blessings," agreed another. "Allah (s.w.t.) has shown us that He is always with us."

"We must tell others about our experience," said one of the youths. "Let us show people the true faith and encourage them to worship Allah (s.w.t.) alone."

And so, the youths spread the message of monotheism and encouraged people to return to Allah (s.w.t.).

The lesson we can **learn** from this story is that we should always believe in Allah (s.w.t.), even when it seems like the whole world is against us. We should remain true to our faith and stay away from bad influences. Allah (s.w.t.) will protect us, watch over us, and stand by us in the most challenging times.

> **Sources:** The Holy Qur'an:
>
> Sura 18, verses 9-26.

HADITH

عن أبي الدرداء عن الرسول صلى الله عليه وسلم قال: مَن حَفِظَ عَشْرَ
آياتٍ مِن أَوَّلِ سُورَةِ الكَهْفِ عُصِمَ مِنَ الدَّجَّالِ

According to Abu Ad-Darda, the Prophet said: "[Whoever] memorizes ten verses from the beginning of Surah Al-Kahf will be saved from the Dajjal."

Muslim 809

DUA

PRAYER FOR THE PROTECTION FROM EVIL ACTS

اللَّهُمَّ إِنِّي أَعُوذُ بكَ مِن شَرِّ ما عَمِلْتُ وَمِنْ شَرِّ ما لَمْ أَعْمَلْ

Allāhumma inni a'ūdhu bika min sharri mä 'amiltu wa-min sharri mä lam a'mal.

Source: Sahih Muslim 2716

O Allah, I seek refuge in You from the evils I have committed and the evils I have not committed.

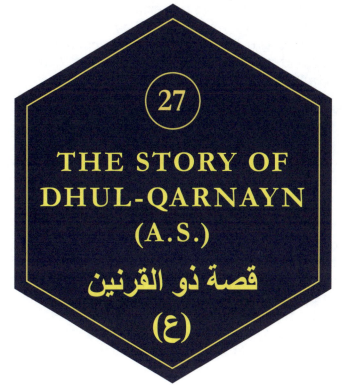

27

THE STORY OF DHUL-QARNAYN (A.S.)

قصة ذو القرنين (ع)

THE STORY OF DHUL-QARNAYN (A.S.)

This is the exciting story of Dhul-Qarnayn (a.s.). Dhul-Qarnayn (a.s.) was a righteous and powerful man - some even believe that he was a king who was endowed by Allah (s.w.t.) with great wisdom and strength. He traveled to many countries and helped people do good and ward off evil on behalf of Allah (s.w.t.). He guided people to the right path.

One day, Dhul-Qarnayn (a.s.) set out on a long journey with his companions and arrived in a country where he met people living in great distress. They asked him for help and pleaded, "O mighty Dhul-Qarnayn (a.s.), please save us from our neighboring peoples who want to threaten and destroy us! In return, we will pay you tribute and submit to you."

Dhul-Qarnayn (a.s.) heard their plea and replied, "Fear not, I will help you and protect you from evil!" With determination in his voice, he said to the people, "We will build a great wall to protect you from your enemies. Everyone lend a hand and bring me iron." Immediately the people ran and brought iron to Dhul-Qarnayn (a.s.). A large fire was lit, and the iron was melted in it. Finally, Dhul-Qarnayn (a.s.) asked the people, "Bring me molten lead so that we can pour it over the iron." So, with the help of Allah (s.w.t.) and His strength, he built a huge wall of iron and lead.

While he was still building the wall, Dhul-Qarnayn (a.s.) called out to his companions, "Let's lay the stones on top of each other and fasten them with great strength and precision!" His voice sounded determined. When the wall was completed, he said, "This is a mercy from my Lord, but when the promise of my Lord comes and He brings judgment on people, He will turn everything to dust; and the promise of my Lord is true." Thus, he reminded the people that all power lies with Allah (s.w.t.). After its completion, the wall was so high and strong that no one could overcome it. It protected the people and brought peace and security to the land.

The story of Dhul-Qarnayn (a.s.) reminds us that it is important to help others in need and to stand up for what is good. We should look for ways to establish peace and security in our world and stand by those who need our support.

> **Sources:** The Holy Qur'an:
>
> Sura 18, verses 83-101.

HADITH

عن أبي هريرة قال: قال رسول الله صلى الله عليه وسلم: .... ولا أدري
ذو القرنين كان نبيا أم لا

Abu Huraira reported the Prophet to have said: "... and I do not know whether Dhul-Qarnayn was a prophet or not."

Source: Ibn Hazm's work
"Al-Muhalla"

DUA

PRAYER FOR SUPPORT AND GUIDANCE

رَبِّ أَعِنِّي وَلَا تُعِنْ عَلَيَّ، وانْصُرْنِي وَلَا تَنْصُرْ عَلَيَّ، وامْكُرْ لِي وَلَا تَمْكُرْ عَلَيَّ،
وَاهْدِنِي وَيَسِّرْ هُدَايَ إِلَيَّ، وَانْصُرْنِي عَلَى مَنْ بَغَى عَلَيَّ، اللَّهُمَّ اجْعَلْنِي لَكَ
شَاكِرًا، لَكَ ذَاكِرًا، لَكَ رَاهِبًا، لَكَ مِطْوَاعًا إِلَيْكَ، مُخْبِتًا، أَوْ مُنِيبًا، رَبِّ تَقَبَّلْ
تَوْبَتِي، وَاغْسِلْ حَوْبَتِي، وَأَجِبْ دَعْوَتِي، وَثَبِّتْ حُجَّتِي، وَاهْدِ قَلْبِي، وَسَدِّدْ لِسَانِي،
وَاسْلُلْ سَخِيمَةَ قَلْبِي

Rabbi a'inni wa-lā tuin 'alayya wa-nsurni wa-lā tansur 'alayya wa-mkur wa-lā tamkur 'alayya wa-hdini wa-yassir hudāya ilayya wa-nsurni 'alā man baghā 'alayya Allāhumma j'alni laka shākiran laka dhākiran laka rāhiban laka mitwā'an ilayka mukhbitan aw muniban rabbi tagabbaltawbati wa-ghsil hawbati wa-ajib da'wati wa-thabbit hujjati wa-hdi galbi wa-saddid lisāni wa-slul sakhimata qalbi.

Source: Jami`
at-Tirmidhi
3551

My Lord, help me, but do not help others against me; support me, but do not support others against me; plan for me, but do not plan against me; guide me rightly and make guidance easy for me. Help me to victory against those who oppress me! O Allah, let me express my gratitude to You and remember You, fear You, be obedient to You, and meet You in humility or repentance! O Lord, accept my repentance and wash away my sins, answer my supplication and strengthen my arguments, guide my heart, direct my tongue, and remove wickedness from my heart.

201

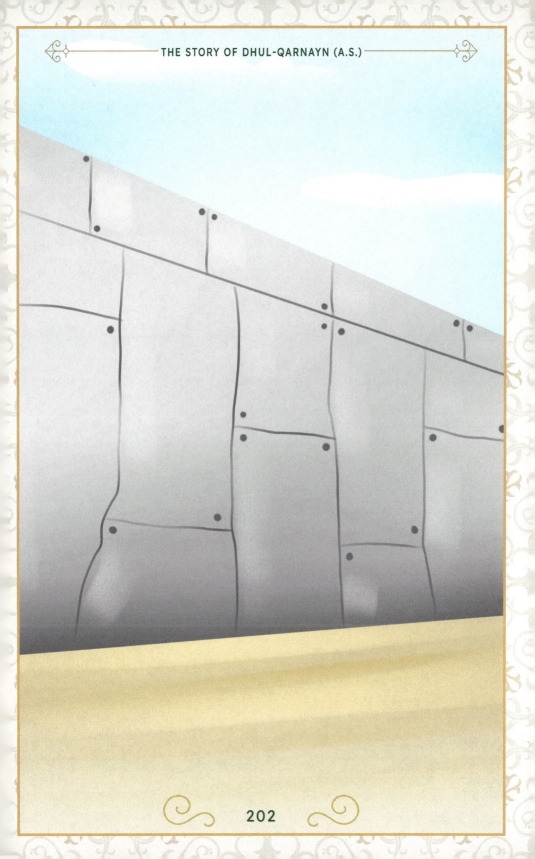

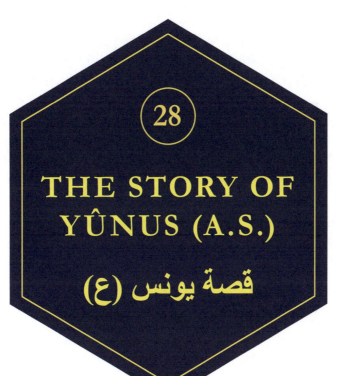

28

THE STORY OF YÛNUS (A.S.)

قصة يونس (ع)

THE STORY OF YÛNUS (A.S.)

In Nineveh, an important city in what was then Assyria, a prophet named Yûnus (a.s.) lived a long time ago. Allah (s.w.t.) chose him to deliver His message to the people and guide them to the right path. Yûnus (a.s.) was a kind and righteous man who always did his best to help his fellow human beings.

One day, however, Yûnus (a.s.) felt disappointed by the people around him. They were disobedient to Allah (s.w.t.) and were living in sin. Yûnus (a.s.) felt that his message was not being heard and his efforts were in vain. Out of despair and disappointment, he left the city and went away without seeking Allah's (s.w.t.) permission first.

Yûnus (a.s.) boarded a ship and set sail. During his journey, the ship was caught in a heavy storm. The sea was raging, and the waves were getting higher and higher. The crew of the ship realized that this storm was a punishment from Allah (s.w.t.) and decided to cast lots to find out who among them was responsible for the storm.

The lot fell on Yûnus (a.s.) and he confessed his offense and his flight from Allah (s.w.t.) to the people on board. The crew threw Yûnus (a.s.) into the sea, whereupon the storm subsided. But Yûnus (a.s.) simply did not sink! Allah (s.w.t.) sent a large fish that swallowed him and kept him safe in its belly. In the darkness of the fish's belly, Yûnus (a.s.) deeply regretted what he had done and asked Allah (s.w.t.) for forgiveness. He realized that he had made a mistake by running away from his responsibility. "O my Lord, in the darkness of the belly of this fish I find myself," Yûnus (a.s.) cried out to Allah (s.w.t.) amidst the narrowness and darkness. "There is no god but You. Praise be to You! Indeed, I have done wrong, and I am ready to change. O Allah (s.w.t.), I turn to You and seek Your mercy!"

Allah (s.w.t.) heard the sincere pleas and repentant words of Yûnus (a.s.). He made the fish swim to a stall and spit out Yûnus (a.s.). He recognized the mercy of Allah (s.w.t.) and vowed never to flee from his duty as a prophet again.

Yûnus (a.s.) returned to Nineveh. Imagine, he stood before the people of Nineveh with a radiant face, and he spoke with a voice full of kindness and wisdom, "Allah (s.w.t.), the Almighty, gave me a second chance and rescued me from the depths of the ocean. We must not forget that His mercy and love are limitless. We must turn to Him and obey His commandments. I was stubborn and neglected my duty, but Allah (s.w.t.) showed me how important it is to be patient and obedient."

He then continued, "Let us come together and pray to Allah (s.w.t.), thank Him for all the blessings He has given us, and strive to be good people. He is merciful and will guide us if we make an honest and sincere effort."

The people of Nineveh listened to Yûnus (a.s.) and began to change their behavior. They prayed to Allah (s.w.t.), asked forgiveness for their sins, and promised to live a righteous and good life. They burned their idols and became helpful people who lived in peace and security.

One day, in a fit of disappointment, Yûnus (a.s.) said, "Why does Allah (s.w.t.) keep forgiving them so quickly?" He felt so disappointed that he decided to leave Nineveh and go to the desert.

When Yûnus (a.s.) was in the desert, he felt the sweltering heat and thirst. Allah (s.w.t.), in His mercy, then made a gourd vine grow over Yûnus (a.s.) to give him shade and protect him from the sun. This shade gave Yûnus (a.s.) comfort and relief in the scorching heat. While he was still sitting under the gourd, Allah (s.w.t.) sent a worm to eat the plant, causing it to wither. Suddenly, Yûnus (a.s.) lost the precious shade and the sun blazed down on him again. He felt abandoned by Allah (s.w.t.).

Allah (s.w.t.) spoke to Yûnus (a.s.) and helped him understand that just as he felt sorrow for the plant that sheltered him, Allah was also concerned about the people of Nineveh. Therefore, Allah

(s.w.t.) treated the people with mercy and forgave them. Yûnus (a.s.) now understood the importance of compassion and patience. He realized the importance of caring for others, not giving up easily, and understanding that Allah's (s.w.t.) mercy and love is for everyone.

The lesson from the story of Yûnus (a.s.) is that we should never run away from our responsibilities. When Allah (s.w.t.) assigns us a task, we should fulfill it with devotion and patience. However, Allah (s.w.t.) is also ready to forgive us if we have committed a mistake and sincerely ask for His forgiveness.

Sources: The Holy Qur'an:

Sura 10, verse 98 | Sura 21, verses 87-88 | Sura 37, verses 139-148 | Sura 68, verses 48-50.

HADITH

عن أبي هريرة رفعه: لما أراد الله حبس يونس في بطن الحوت، أمر الله الحوت أنْ لا يكسر له عظماً، ولا يخدش له لحماً فلما انتهى به إلى قعر ا لبحر

According to Abu Huraira, when Allah decided to keep Yûnus in the whale's belly, He commanded the whale not to break its bones and not to inflict flesh wounds on it. When he was brought to the bottom of the sea...

Fath Al-Bari 6/542

DUA

PRAYER FOR JUST PUNISHMENTS FOR WEALTHY SINNERS

رَبَّنَا ٱطْمِسْ عَلَىٰ أَمْوَٰلِهِمْ وَٱشْدُدْ عَلَىٰ قُلُوبِهِمْ فَلَا يُؤْمِنُوا۟ حَتَّىٰ يَرَوُا۟ ٱلْعَذَابَ ٱلْأَلِيمَ

Rabbanā ṭmis ʿalā 'amwālihim wa-šdud ʿalā qulūbihim fa-lā yu'minū ḥattā yarawu l-ʿaḏāba l- 'alīma.

Our Lord, destroy their riches and strike their hearts so that they will not believe before they experience the painful punishment.

Source: Sura 10:88 (yūnus)

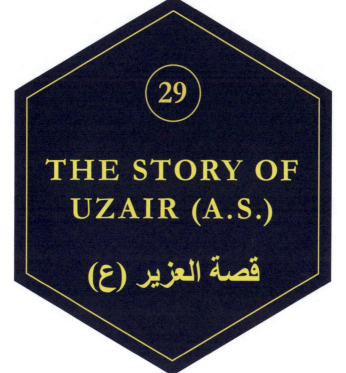

29

THE STORY OF UZAIR (A.S.)

قصة العزير (ع)

THE STORY OF UZAIR (A.S.)

Uzair (a.s.) was a righteous and wise man who lived with the Bani Israel. He was a scribe and teacher who studied the law of God and helped people to understand it. Uzair (a.s.) was known for his piety and his efforts to spread the teachings of Allah (s.w.t.).

One day, however, Uzair (a.s.) was expelled from the city because he had called on the rulers to give up their idolatry. From then on, he lived in the desert until he received instructions from Allah (s.w.t.) to visit his hometown of Jerusalem. Jerusalem was destroyed at that time. But Uzair (a.s.) was to rebuild the city to give the people back their strength and faith.

So Uzair (a.s.) began his journey to Jerusalem, taking a donkey with him as a means of transportation. On the way, however, he found a harrowing scene, A village just outside Jerusalem had been destroyed and the people and animals were dead. Uzair (a.s.) was shocked and lost his faith in the rebuilding of Jerusalem.

In this moment of despair and doubt, Allah (s.w.t.) took Uzair (a.s.) into a deep sleep. This lasted for 100 years. During this time, Allah (s.w.t.) protected him and did not allow him to age. At the end of this time, Allah (s.w.t.) brought Uzair (a.s.) back to life and the donkey, which had previously turned to dust, also came back to life. Allah (s.w.t.) simply reassembled the donkey's bones and covered them with flesh and skin.

When Uzair (a.s.) woke, he felt that a long time had passed, although it had seemed like only a moment to him. He was amazed at the changes around him. He set off for Jerusalem. The city had blossomed, the temple had been rebuilt and the people had returned to the true faith. It was a sign of the mercy of Allah (s.w.t.) that He had rebuilt the city. Uzair (a.s.) deeply regretted his doubt and vowed to dedicate his life to Allah (s.w.t.) and continue to support the people in their faith. He called out to Allah (s.w.t.), "Allah (s.w.t.), my Lord! How is this possible? The city has been restored and the people have regained their faith. You are indeed the Almighty!"

Uzair (a.s.) realized that Allah (s.w.t.) has the power to change even the most hopeless situations. He deeply regretted his doubts. He continued to teach people the commandments of Allah (s.w.t.) and encouraged them to worship Him and always live in unity and peace.

The story of Uzair (a.s.) teaches us that Allah (s.w.t.) has the power to change even the most hopeless situations. It reminds us that we should never lose our faith and always trust in His mercy. If we keep our faith and endure our trials with patience and humility, Allah (s.w.t.) will reward us.

> **Sources:** The Holy Qur'an:
>
> Sura 2, verse 259.

HADITH

قال الشيخ عبد المحسن العباد حفظه الله : وهذا قاله صلى الله عليه وسلم
...، وأما عزير: فلم يأت شيء يدل على أنه نبي

Shaykh 'Abd al-Muhsin al-Abbad (may Allah be pleased with him) reported: "The Prophet said: 'As for Uzair, there is no evidence that he was a prophet. '"

Sunan Abi Dawood 26/468

DUA

PRAYER TO EASE THE SORROW

اللَّهمَّ لا سَهْلَ إِلَّا ما جعَلْتَه سَهلًا وأنتَ تجعلُ الحَزْنَ سَهلًا إذا شِئْتَ

Allāhumma la sahla illā mā ja'altahu sahlan, wa-anta taj'alu l-hazna idhā shi'ta sahlan.

O Allah, there is nothing easy except that which You have made easy, and if You will, You make grief easy.

*Ibn As-Sunni in
'Aml al-Yawm
wa'l-Laylah
(351)*

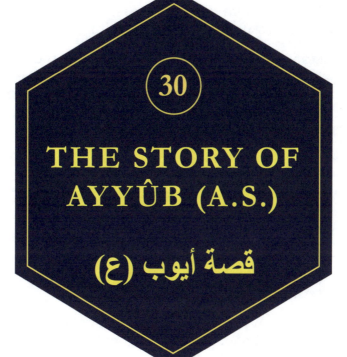

30

THE STORY OF AYYÛB (A.S.)

قصة أيوب (ع)

THE STORY OF AYYÛB (A.S.)

Ayyûb (a.s.) was a sincere and God-fearing man who lived in a land called Uz. He had a loving family and was blessed by Allah (s.w.t.) with wealth and happiness, but one day Iblîs, the devil, wanted to dissuade him from his faith.

Iblîs sent various trials upon Ayyûb (a.s.) one after the other. First, he destroyed his crops so that Ayyûb (a.s.) lost his wealth. But Ayyûb (a.s.) remained patient and said, "Allah (s.w.t.) has given me and He has taken from me. Everything is from Him, and He knows best what is good for me."

Next, Iblîs sent a great tragedy upon Ayyûb (a.s.) and his family. His children were killed in an accident, and he lost them, but Ayyûb (a.s.) remained steadfast in his faith and said, "Allah (s.w.t.) has given them to me and He has taken them to Himself. May He bless her and give me the strength to overcome this trial."

After that, Ayyûb (a.s.) became ill and was in a bad way. Nevertheless, he continued to hold on to his faith. His wife took care of him while he lay in bed and rested.

Then Iblîs incited Ayyûb's (a.s.) wife to dissuade him from faith and advise him to abandon Allah (s.w.t.), but Ayyûb (a.s.) rebuked her and reminded her of the virtues of patience and firm faith in Allah (s.w.t.). He said to her, "When I feel better, I will punish you with 100 strokes of the cane. You should not have listened to God's enemy!"

Allah (s.w.t.) saw the patience and firm faith of Ayyûb (a.s.) and decided to reward him for it, by curing his illness. Instead of the 100 blows with a stick, Ayyûb's (a.s.) wife received only one blow with a bundle of straw. Allah (s.w.t.) wanted to show that He rewards the patience of Ayyûb (a.s.) and his steadfastness and turns the harsh punishment into a gentle one. He also gave his faithful Ayyûb (a.s.) three daughters and seven sons, twice as much wealth as before, and blessed him with a long, happy life.

The story of Ayyûb (a.s.) teaches us that even in the most challenging times, patience and faith can help us to overcome our trials, and even when we are seriously ill, not to lose our faith. We should not be dissuaded by the temptations of the devil and should always trust in the mercy and reward of Allah (s.w.t.).

Sources: The Holy Qur'an:

Sura 21, verses 83-84 | Sura 38, verses 41-44.

HADITH

بَيْنَما أَيُّوبُ يَغْتَسِلُ عُرْيانًا خَرَّ عليه رجْلُ جَرادٍ مِن ذَهَبٍ، فَجَعَلَ يَحْثِي
في ثَوْبِهِ، فَنادَى رَبُّهُ: يا أَيُّوبُ أَلَمْ أَكُنْ أَغْنَيْتُكَ عَمَّا تَرَى؟ قالَ: بَلَى، يا
رَبِّ، ولَكِنْ لا غِنَى بي عن بَرَكَتِكَ

When Ayyûb was washing himself naked, a large amount of gold fell on him. He started to pick it up, but then Allah called him, "O Ayyûb, have I not provided for you beyond your needs?" He replied, "Yes, my Lord, nothing can exempt me from Your blessings."

Sahih al-Bukhari 7493

DUA

PRAYER FOR SUPPORT IN DIFFICULT SITUATIONS

أَنِّي مَسَّنِيَ ٱلضُّرُّ وَأَنتَ أَرْحَمُ ٱلرَّاحِمِين

'Annī massaniya ḍ-ḍurru wa-'anta 'arḥamu r- rāḥimīna.

I am afflicted by misfortune, and You are the most merciful of the merciful.

Source:
Sura 21:83
(al-'anbiyā')

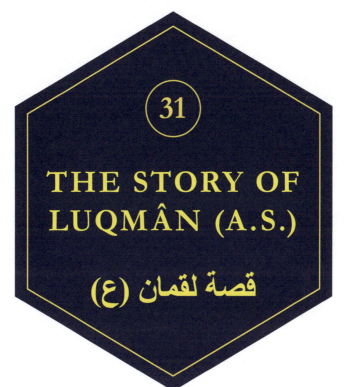

31

THE STORY OF
LUQMÂN (A.S.)

قصة لقمان (ع)

THE STORY OF LUQMÂN (A.S.)

Luqmân (a.s.) was a wise man to whom Allah (s.w.t.) had bestowed exceptional wisdom and insight. He was a good and God-fearing man who treated the people around him with love and kindness.

One day, Luqmân (a.s.) turned to his son and said, "My dear son, I would like to give you some important advice that will help you lead a good and fulfilling life. Listen carefully and learn from my words."

Luqmân (a.s.) continued and said, "My son, serve Allah (s.w.t.) and keep His commandments. Avoid disbelief and the wrong path. Be grateful for the blessings Allah (s.w.t.) has given you and show compassion and kindness to the people around you."

He also told his son a story about an ant that was wise and exercised caution when King Sulaimân (a.s.) passed by them. Luqmân (a.s.) said, "Imagine this ant, my son. Although it is small, it plans its work carefully and gathers provisions for the future. Learn from it that you should always look ahead."

Luqmân (a.s.) also admonished his son to do good deeds and stay away from bad habits. He explained to him that speaking the truth and keeping promises are important to gain people's trust. Luqmân (a.s.) emphasized that parents should be honored and respected because they had made great sacrifices for their children.

Luqmân (a.s.) also taught his son the importance of knowledge and education. He said: "My son, strive for knowledge and education. Learn from the scholars and always be curious and inquisitive. Because knowledge will guide you and make you a better person."

He concluded his words with special advice, "My son, be modest and humble. Arrogance and haughtiness will only distance you from Allah (s.w.t.). Be patient in times of trial and grateful in times of happiness."

The lesson from the story of Luqmân (a.s.) is that wisdom, God-fearing actions, gratitude, and humility lead us to a fulfilled life. We should accept the advice of the wise and strive to live a life according to the teachings of Islam. We should also treat our parents with love and always honor them.

Sources: The Holy Qur'an:

Sura 31, verses 12-19.

HADITH

وقد قال البخاري : حدثنا قتيبة حدثنا جرير عن الأعمش عن إبراهيم
عن علقمة عن عبد الله قال لما نزلت الذين آمنوا ولم يلبسوا إيمانهم
بظلم [الأنعام : ٨٢] شق ذلك على أصحاب رسول الله صلى الله عليه
وسلم ، وقالوا : أينا لم يلبس إيمانه بظلم ؟ فقال رسول الله صلى الله
عليه وسلم : إنه ليس بذاك ألم تسمع إلى قول لقمان ؟ يابني لا تشرك
بالله إن الشرك لظلم عظيم [لقمان : ١٣] ورواه مسلم

Imam al-Bukhari reported that Qatada said, after Jarir, after al-A'mash, after Ibrâhîm, after 'Alqama, after Abdullah, who said, "When the verse 'Those who believe and have not disturbed the purity of their faith by injustice' (Al-An'am 82) was revealed, it troubled the Companions of the Prophet, and they said, 'We are those who believe.' They asked: 'Who among us has not disturbed his faith by an injustice? , The Prophet replied: 'It is not that. Have you not heard the words of Luqmân: 'O my son, do not associate Allah with [another god], for indeed, association is a great injustice<' (Luqmân 13)" (Reported by Muslim).

Tafsir Ibn Kathir, 412

DUA

PRAYER TO SUCCESSFULLY COMPLETE
THE EXAM PREPARATION

اللهم افتح علي أبواب حكمتك وانشر علي رحمتك وامنن علي بالحفظ
والفهم سبحانك لا علم لنا إلا ما علمتنا إنك أنت العليم الحكيم

Allāhumma aftah li 'abwab hikmatika, wanshur ely rahmataka, wamnina ealayun bialhifz walfahmu, subhanak la eilm lana 'iilaa ma ealimatana, 'iinak 'ant alealim alhakimu.

Source: Sahih Muslim

O Allah, open for me the doors of Your wisdom, spread Your mercy over me, and grant me learning and understanding, glory be to You. We have no knowledge except what You have taught us, for You are the All-Knowing, the Wise.

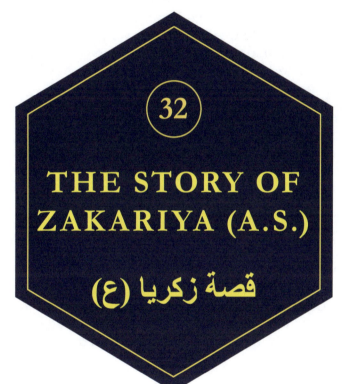

32

THE STORY OF ZAKARIYA (A.S.)

قصة زكريا (ع)

THE STORY OF ZAKARIYA (A.S.)

This is the encouraging story of Zakariya (a.s.), who lived in a time when people had once again strayed from the right path. They had forgotten to worship Allah (s.w.t.) and were living in sin and injustice; worshipping idols and drinking wine. Zakariya (a.s.) though, remained steadfast in his faith and served Allah (s.w.t.) with all his heart.

One day, when Zakariya (a.s.) had reached old age and his wife was barren, he felt a deep longing for a child. He wanted so much to have an offspring who would carry his message and lead the people on the right path. He knelt and turned to Allah (s.w.t.) in deep humility, "My Lord, grant me from You a pure offspring."

Then suddenly an angel appeared to him in the form of a human being. The angel announced the good news to Zakariya (a.s.), "O Zakariya (a.s.), Allah (s.w.t.) gives you the good news of a son named Yahya (a.s.). He will be the first of his name." Zakariya (a.s.) was overwhelmed with joy and gratitude to Allah (s.w.t.). He replied in astonishment, "My Lord, how can I have a son when my wife is barren, and I have already reached an old age?" The angel answered him, "Do not worry. Allah (s.w.t.) creates what He wills."

With a joyful heart, Zakariya (a.s.) rushed to his wife and told her the good news. Together they looked forward to the imminent birth of their son. Zakariya (a.s.) felt the deep blessing and grace of Allah (s.w.t.) in his life. He was grateful for the fulfillment of his wish and knew that Allah (s.w.t.) was always there to answer our prayers.

The people around Zakariya (a.s.) were astonished at the fulfillment of his wish and recognized the power and mercy of Allah (s.w.t.). They were reminded that Allah (s.w.t.) rewards those who serve Him sincerely and trust in Him. Yahya (a.s.) studied the commandments of Allah (s.w.t.), spread His message, and served Him together with his parents.

The lesson from the story of Zakariya (a.s.) is that we should never give up hope and always turn to Allah (s.w.t.) because He has the power to make everything possible. Allah (s.w.t.) is the only One who answers prayers, and He knows our innermost desires and needs.

Sources: The Holy Qur'an:

Sura 3, verses 37-41 | Sura 21, verses 90-91.

HADITH

قال الإمام أحمد: حدثنا يزيد - يعني ابن هرون - أنبأنا حماد بن سلمة،
عن ثابت، عن أبي رافع، عن أبي هريرة، أن رسول الله ﷺ قال: كان
زكريا نجارا

Imam Ahmad said, "Yazid, i.e. ibn Harun, reported to us, Hammad ibn Salama reported to us from Thabit, Abu Rafi' and Abu Huraira that the Prophet (s.a.w.) said, 'Zakariya was a carpenter.'"

So, Muslim reported, and
Ibn Majah reported from
Hammad ibn Salama

DUA

PRAYER FOR SUCCESS IN THIS WORLD AND IN THE HEREAFTER

رَبَّنَآ ءَاتِنَا فِي ٱلدُّنْيَا حَسَنَةً وَفِي ٱلْأَخِرَةِ حَسَنَةً وَقِنَا عَذَابَ ٱلنَّارِ

Rabbana atina fi ddunya hasanah wa fi lakhirati hasanah wa qina 'adhaba an-nar.

O Allah, give us the good of this world and the good of the Hereafter, and save us from the punishment of Hell.

Source: Surat
Al-Baqarah
(2:201)

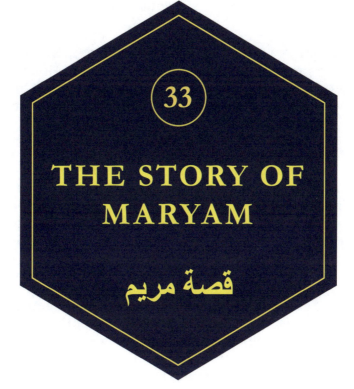

33

THE STORY OF MARYAM

قصة مريم

THE STORY OF MARYAM

This is the beautiful story of Maryam. Before we start telling her fascinating life story, we would like to tell you about her mother.

Maryam's mother was a devout woman who desperately wanted a child. She prayed to Allah (s.w.t.) and implored Him for a son. In her deep humility, she turned to Him and promised that if her wish for a child was granted, she would dedicate them exclusively to Allah (s.w.t.) and raise them in His service.

One day, her prayers were answered, and she gave birth to a child. It was a beautiful girl, whom she named Maryam. Earlier, when she realized that her child was not a boy but a girl, she initially felt a certain surprise. But she was a woman of faith and devotion, so she turned to Allah (s.w.t.) with confidence in her heart and said, "O my Lord, I have given birth to a girl, and the female is not equal to the male. I have named her Maryam and I ask You to protect her and her offspring from the influence of evil."

She fulfilled her promise and raised Maryam in deep devotion to Allah (s.w.t.). Maryam grew up to be an exceptionally virtuous and God-fearing woman. She lived a secluded life and devoted herself to the study of her faith. Her guardian was none other than Zakariya (a.s.), the venerable prophet and scholar. Zakariya (a.s.) was impressed by Maryam's extraordinary devotion and virtue. He recognized her special closeness to Allah (s.w.t.) and knew that she would play an important role in His plan. He became her teacher and began to instruct her in the teachings of faith and righteousness. Zakariya (a.s.) observed Maryam's extraordinary piety and the grace that Allah (s.w.t.) had poured upon her. He saw her engrossed in her worship and humbly prostrated before Allah (s.w.t.). Through his wisdom and guidance, he helped her to further her spiritual development and understand her special role in the service of Allah (s.w.t.). She spent much time in prayer and worship and found inner peace in her relationship with Allah (s.w.t.).

Lesson from the story of Maryam: This story teaches us that Allah (s.w.t.) will always support those who sincerely serve and trust Him. It reminds us that true strength and fulfillment lies in obedience to Allah (s.w.t.) and humility before His will.

Sources: The Holy Qur'an:

Sura 3, verses 35-37 | Sura 19, verses 16-40 | Sura 21, verse 91 | Sura 19, verses 16-40 | Sura 21, verse 91.

HADITH

قال صلى الله عليه وسلم: حسبك من نساء العالمين: مريم ابنة عمران,
وخديجة بنت خويلد, وفاطمة بنت محمد, وآسية امرأة فرعون

The Prophet Muhammad (s.a.w.) said: "The best women in the world are
Maryam, the daughter of Imran, Khadija, the daughter of Khuwaylid,
Fatima, the daughter of Muhammad, and Asiya, the wife of Pharaoh."

Sahih al-Bukhari 3432

DUA

PRAYERS FOR STIMULATION AND SELF-MOTIVATION

رَبِّ أَوْزِعْنِي أَنْ أَشْكُرَ نِعْمَتَكَ ٱلَّتِي أَنْعَمْتَ عَلَيَّ وَعَلَىٰ وَٰلِدَيَّ وَأَنْ أَعْمَلَ
صَٰلِحًا تَرْضَىٰهُ وَأَصْلِحْ لِي فِي ذُرِّيَّتِيٓ إِنِّي تُبْتُ إِلَيْكَ وَإِنِّي مِنَ ٱلْمُسْلِمِينَ

Rabbi 'awzi'nī 'an 'aškura
ni'mataka llatī 'an'amta
'alayya wa-'alā wālidayya
wa-'an 'a'mala ṣāliḥan
tarḍāhu wa-'aṣliḥ lī fī
ḍurriyyatī 'innī tubtu 'ilayka
wa-'innī mina l- muslimīna

Source:
Sura 46:15
(al-'aḥqāf)

My Lord, spur me on to be
grateful for Your grace that
You have shown me and my
parents, and (spur me on
to) work righteousness that
may please You. And let my
descendants be righteous.
Behold, I turn to You, and I
am one of the devoted.

34

MARYAM AND 'ÎSA (A.S.)

مريم وعيسى (ع)

MARYAM AND 'ÎSA (A.S.)

One day, the angel Jibril appeared to Maryam in the form of a human being. Maryam was frightened at first, but he calmed her down and said, "Do not be afraid, for I am a messenger of Allah (s.w.t.). He has chosen you and made you pure and full of virtue."

Jibrīl gave Maryam an extraordinary message, she would conceive a child even though she had not yet married. Maryam was astonished and asked, "How can I have a child when no man has touched me?" The angel replied, "That's right. You will give birth to a son without having been touched by a man. This son will be called 'Îsa (a.s.). Allah (s.w.t.) creates what He wills. When He decides a thing, He only says 'Become' and it becomes." Jibrīl also indicated the special life and mission that 'Îsa (a.s.) would have. He said to Maryam, "Maryam, 'Îsa (a.s.) the Messiah will be honored in this world and the Hereafter and will be one of the closest to Allah (s.w.t.). He will speak to people as a child and as an adult and he will be one of the righteous."

Through these words, we know that 'Îsa (a.s.) was to lead an incredibly special life from the very beginning. He was to bring the word of Allah (s.w.t.) to the people, both as a child and as an adult, and he would be a prophet, someone chosen by Allah (s.w.t.) to proclaim His message.

But back to Maryam. She felt deep humility and submission to the will of Allah (s.w.t.). She accepted the message and prepared herself to receive the special child. During this time, she withdrew to a remote area to completely surrender to Allah (s.w.t.). She found refuge in the desert and there, under a date palm, she went into labor.

The birth of a child can be very painful, and Maryam was alone. She wished she had never been born herself. After giving birth, Maryam was exhausted and thirsty and did not know what to do, but in this moment of deep despair, Allah (s.w.t.) spoke to her. He told her not to be afraid and to shake the trunk of the date palm.

When Maryam shook the tree, ripe, sweet dates fell from it. She was able to eat them and gain strength and energy. And that was not all. Allah (s.w.t.) caused a small stream to spring up at her feet. She was able to wash her face in it and quench her thirst. She felt better and found strength thanks to Allah's (s.w.t.) help, who took care of her and little Îsa (a.s.).

Finally, Maryam returned to her relatives. They were surprised and did not believe that 'Îsa (a.s.) had been born without a father. They reproached Maryam severely. They said, "Maryam, your parents were good people, how could you do such a thing?" Maryam, who remembered Allah's (s.w.t.) message, did not speak but pointed to her baby. And to her surprise, little 'Îsa (a.s.) spoke. He said, "I am indeed the servant of Allah (s.w.t.). He has made me His Prophet. He has blessed me wherever I am and has imposed prayer on me for as long as I live."

People were amazed, a talking baby was a miracle! They realized that Allah (s.w.t.) played a role in this event. From that moment on, they respected Maryam and her child and saw in 'Îsa (a.s.) a special sign from Allah (s.w.t.).

One day, when 'Îsa (a.s.) was still a child, he was playing outside and made some birds out of mud. This was on a Sabbath, a day on which work was suspended and is still suspended in certain regions of the world. The people around him were astonished and said, "'Îsa (a.s.), you should not work on the Sabbath! It is a holy day."

Then 'Îsa (a.s.) did something truly amazing. He breathed life into the birds made of mud and they flew away! The people were amazed and could hardly believe what they saw. This was another sign that 'Îsa (a.s.) was a special prophet whom Allah (s.w.t.) had blessed with special abilities.

The story of Maryam and 'Îsa (a.s.) teaches us many things. It shows us to always have faith in Allah (s.w.t.), no matter how difficult or inexplicable the situation may seem. It also shows us that Allah (s.w.t.) blesses those who serve Him faithfully and piously.

> **Sources:** The Holy Qur'an:
>
> Sura 3, verses 45-47 | Sura 19, verse 33 | Sura 43, verse 61.

HADITH

ما مِن مولودٍ يُولَدُ إِلَّا يَمَسُّه الشَّيطانُ فيَستَهِلُّ صارِخًا إِلَّا مريمَ ابنةَ عِمرانَ وابنَها، إِن شِئتُم اقرَؤوا : إِنِّي أُعيذُها بِكَ وَذُرِّيَّتَها مِنَ الشَّيطانِ الرَّجيمِ

"Every newborn child is touched by Satan as soon as it is born, and it utters a shrill cry, with the exception of Mary, the daughter of Imran, and her son. If you wish, you can recite: 'I place her and her offspring under your protection from the exiled devil' (Surah Al-Imran 3:36)."

Sahih Ibn Hibban 6235

DUA

PRAYER FOR ADVICE AND HELP

اللَّهُمَّ إِنِّي أَسْتَخِيرُكَ بِعِلْمِكَ، وَأَسْتَقْدِرُكَ بِقُدْرَتِكَ، وَأَسْأَلُكَ مِن فَضْلِكَ الْعَظِيمِ فَإِنَّكَ تَقْدِرُ وَلا أَقْدِرُ، وَتَعْلَمُ وَلا أَعْلَمُ، وَأَنْتَ عَ عَ امُ الْغُيُوبِ.. اللَّهُمَّ إِنْ كُنْتَ تَعْلَمُ أَنَّ هَذَا ا الأَمْرَ خَيْرٌ لِي فِي دِينِي وَمَعَاشِي وَعَاقِبَةِ أَمْرِي؛ فَاقْدُرْهُ ل ل لِي وَيَسِّرْهُ لِي ثُمَّ بَارِكْ لِي فِيهِ.. اللَّهُمَّ وَإِنْ كُنْتَ تَعْلَمُ أَنَّ هَذَا ا ا الأَمْرَ شَرَ لِي فِي دِينِي وَمَعَاشِي وَعَاقِبَةِ أَمْرِي لَّ فَاصْرِفْهُ عَنِّي وَاصْرِفْنِي عَنْهُ وَاقْدُرْ لِي الْخَيْرَ حَيْثُ كَانَ ثُمَّ ارْضِنِي بِهِ

Allāhumma inni astakhiru-kabi- ilmika wa-astagdiruka bi-qudratika, wa-as'aluka min fadlika l-'adhimi, fa-innaka tag-diru wa-lā agdiru wa-talamu wa-lā allamu, wa-anta 'allāmu l-ghuyūbi, allāhumma in kunta ta'lamu anna hādhā l-amra khayrun Ii fi dini wa-ma'ashi wa-'āgibati amri fa-qdurhu li wa-yassirhu I thumma bārik li fihi, Allāhumma wa-in kunta ta'lamu anna hādhā l-amra sharrun li fi dini wa-ma'āshi wa-āgibati amri fa-srifhu 'anni wa-srifni 'anhu, wa-qdur lil-khayra haythu kāna thumma ardini bihi.

Source: Sahih al-Bukhari 1166 (6019)

O Allah, I ask You for the right decision through Your knowledge; I ask You for strength (to carry out the plan) through Your power, and I ask You for Your great favor. You are able and I am not. You know and I do not know, and You know the hidden! O Allah! If You know that this matter is good for me, for my faith, for my way of life, and for my Hereafter (or say: If it is better for my present and future needs), then determine it for me and make it easier for me, and then give me Your blessing on it! But if you know that this matter is bad for me, for my faith, for my way of life, and for my hereafter (or say: If it is bad for my present and future needs), then keep it away from me and keep me away from it! Determine good for me, wherever it may be, and then make me content with it!

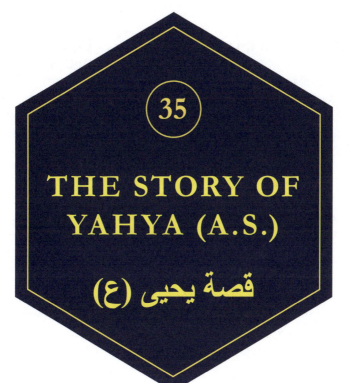

35

THE STORY OF YAHYA (A.S.)

قصة يحيى (ع)

THE STORY OF YAHYA (A.S.)

Do you remember Yahya (a.s.), the son of Zakariya (a.s.)? This is his story.

Yahya (a.s.) was known for his kindness and justice. He spoke the truth, even if it was sometimes difficult to hear. And he called people to confess to Allah (s.w.t.) and repent of their sins. Yahya (a.s.) was also known for his great modesty. He lived very simply, wore clothes made of camel's hair, and fed on wild honey and locusts. He led a simple life because he believed that it was more important to spend time praying and teaching people than striving for material wealth.

He said to the idol worshippers, "You should worship Allah (s.w.t.) alone. These idols you worship can neither help nor harm you. Only Allah (s.w.t.) is the One who deserves to be worshipped."

One of the people to whom Yahya (a.s.) told the truth was a powerful and evil king named Herod. Herod ruled brutally and had many people murdered. Yahya (a.s.) criticized Herod for his sins, his unjust behavior, and his lavish lifestyle. "Herod, you are acting unjustly and against the commandments of Allah (s.w.t.). You should only worship Allah (s.w.t.) and obey His commandments. Your deeds are wrong, you should mend your ways and ask for forgiveness. Only Allah (s.w.t.) is the rightful God and Judge, and we should all obey and worship Him." The king though, did not want to hear the truth and was angry with Yahya (a.s.). So, he threw him into a dungeon, a dark and cold place.

But even there, Yahya (a.s.) did not give up his faith in Allah (s.w.t.). He continued to pray and trusted that He would protect him. Then Yahya (a.s.) was executed by King Herod. So, Herod wanted to silence Yahya (a.s.) forever. Yet even in those dark moments, Yahya (a.s.) never lost his faith or hope in Allah (s.w.t.). He knew

 251

that he, like every other human being, would one day return to Allah (s.w.t.). This is something he had told people over and over again. He said, "I am just a human being like you. I will die one day and return to our Creator, Allah (s.w.t.)."

The words of Yahya (a.s.) helped people not to lose their faith despite the challenging times.

This story shows us that we should be courageous and steadfast in our faith, just as Yahya (a.s.) was. We should always tell the truth, live modestly, and focus on what is important in life: our faith in Allah (s.w.t.) and supporting other people.

Sources: The Holy Qur'an:

Sura 6, verse 85 | Sura 19, verses 12-15 | Sura 21, verses 90-91.

HADITH

وقد جاء في الحديث قوله صلى الله عليه وسلم: لا ينبغي لأحد أن يقول: أنا خير من يحيى بن زكريا, قلنا: يا رسول الله! ومن أين ذاك؟ قال: أما سمعتم الله كيف وصفه في القرآن, فقال: {يا يحيى خذ الكتاب بقوة وآتيناه الحكم صبيا} فقرأ حتى بلغ: {وسيدا وحصورا ونبيا من الصالحين} لم يعمل سيئة قط, ولم يهم بها

In this hadith, the Prophet Muhammad (s.a.w.) said: "It is not appropriate for anyone to say that he is better than Yahya ibn Zakariya." We asked him, "O Messenger of Allah, where does this come from?" He replied, "Have you not heard Allah describing him in the Qur'an and saying, 'O Yahya, take the Book with power' (Maryam 19:12). He read until he reached the passage: 'He is a master, chaste and a prophet among the righteous' (Al-Imran 3:39) He never committed a bad deed or even thought of doing it."

Narrated by At-Tabarani in Al-Kabir and Al-Bazzar

DUA

PRAYER FOR KNOWLEDGE AND ITS PROPER APPLICATION

اللَّهُمَّ انْفَعْنِي بِمَا عَلَّمْتَنِي، وَعَلِّمْنِي مَا يَنْفَعُنِي، وَزِدْنِي عِلْمًا

Allāhumma-n-fa'ni bima 'allamtani, wa 'allimni ma yan-fa'uni, wa zidni 'ilm.

O Allah! Grant me benefit in what You have taught me and teach me useful knowledge and increase my knowledge.

Source: Sunan At-Tirmidhi

36

'ÎSA (A.S.)
TEACHES
PEOPLE

عيسى (ع) يعلم الناس

'ÎSA (A.S.) TEACHES PEOPLE

When 'Îsa (a.s.), the son of Maryam, grew up, he lived a very modest life. He did not have wealth, a large house, or many possessions. Instead, he focused on spreading Allah's (s.w.t.) message and helping people. He traveled through the country, ate wild fruits and wore modest clothing.

One day, 'Îsa (a.s.) stood before a large crowd and spoke to them. He said, "I have been sent by Allah (s.w.t.) to deliver His message to you."

He urged them to live in modesty, honesty, and freedom and to always be ready to help.

Then 'Îsa (a.s.) asked, "Which of you would like to be my helper to spread Allah's (s.w.t.) message?" 12 men came forward and agreed to help him. They became his disciples and followed him wherever he went. They also lived as modestly as 'Îsa (a.s.).

Together they told people about Allah's (s.w.t.) love and kindness. They helped the poor and prayed together. 'Îsa (a.s.) had the gift of healing the sick and he used this gift to help the needy and alleviate their suffering. Once 'Îsa (a.s.) met a blind man. He had not been able to see since birth, but 'Îsa (a.s.) placed his hands on the man's eyes and prayed to Allah (s.w.t.). And do you know what? The blind man could suddenly see! He was overjoyed to finally be able to see the world and thanked 'Îsa (a.s.) and Allah (s.w.t.) for this miracle.

These were not the only miracles that 'Îsa (a.s.) performed, he even brought a man back from the dead!

Not all people were happy about what 'Îsa (a.s.) was doing. The scholars in the temple became jealous of 'Îsa (a.s.). They feared for their power and influence and were afraid that people would soon stop listening to them. The scholars thought about how they could get rid of 'Îsa (a.s.).

One day, 'Îsa (a.s.) spoke in front of a large crowd, including his disciples and some of the temple scholars. 'Îsa (a.s.) said, "Purify your hearts and keep Allah (s.w.t.) always in your thoughts. Do not brag about your actions and do not pray only to be seen and admired by others. Rather, be humble and modest. Always remember that you are facing Allah (s.w.t.) during prayer and that He sees and hears you. Support the needy in secret and do not do it just to be called generous by others. When you fast, do not appear sad, but wear clean clothes, comb your hair, and be cheerful so that only Allah (s.w.t.) knows that you are fasting. Avoid meaningless and unnecessary talk. Be honest and do not deceive yourselves or others. Allah (s.w.t.) knows all the hidden things in heaven and earth and is aware of what is hidden in your hearts. One day you will have to give an account to Him."

'Îsa (a.s.) talked for many hours and evening had come. The crowd had forgotten to eat, and many had to walk a long way home. Therefore, the listeners asked 'Îsa (a.s.) for something to eat. 'Îsa (a.s.) prayed to Allah (s.w.t.) and He sent a table full of food from heaven. There was enough for everyone, and the poor satisfied their hunger; those who did not believe in the word of 'Îsa (a.s.) did not eat any of the food that Allah (s.w.t.) had sent. And the scholars still did not believe the wise words. They thought that it was a trick or a spell and refused to acknowledge that 'Îsa (a.s.) had been sent by Allah (s.w.t.). Rather, they were now even more jealous of him.

The story of 'Îsa (a.s.) teaches us steadfastness in faith. It also teaches us the importance of modesty and helping those in need. And it reminds us that Allah (s.w.t.) is always ready to support us when we ask Him for help.

Sources: The Holy Qur'an:

Sura 3, verses 49-53 | Sura 5, verse 19 | Sura 5, verses 49-50 | Sura 5, verses 113-121 | Sura 9, verse 30 | Sura 19, verses 30-33.

HADITH

رُوِيَ عَنِ النبيِّ (صلى الله عليه و آله) أنَّهُ قَالَ : إِنَّ عِيسَى ابْنَ مَرْيَمَ (عليه السلام) قَامَ فِي بَنِي إِسْرَائِيلَ فَقَالَ : يَا بَنِي إِسْرَائِيلَ ، لَا تُحَدِّثُوا بِالْحِكْمَةِ الْجُهَّالَ فَتَظْلِمُوهَا ، وَ لَا تَمْنَعُوهَا أَهْلَهَا فَتَظْلِمُوهُمْ ، وَ لَا تُعِينُوا الظَّالِمَ عَلَى ظُلْمِهِ فَيَبْطُلَ فَضْلُكُمْ

It is narrated that the Prophet Muhammad (s.a.w.) said: "Verily, ʿĪsa, the son of Maryam, stood up among the Children of Israel and said: 'O Children of Israel, do not impart wisdom to the ignorant, lest you corrupt them. And do not withhold it from those who are worthy of it, lest you oppress them. And do not support the oppressor in his injustice, or your favor will be invalid.'"

Sheikh Muhammad Baqir al-Majlisi, Bihar al-Anwar: 14/349

DUA

PRAYER FOR RIGHTEOUSNESS AND GRATITUDE

رَبِّ أَوْزِعْنِي أَنْ أَشْكُرَ نِعْمَتَكَ ٱلَّتِي أَنْعَمْتَ عَلَيَّ وَعَلَىٰ وُلِدَيَّ وَأَنْ أَعْمَلَ صُلِحًا تَرْضَىٰهُ وَأَدْخِلْنِي بِرَحْمَتِكَ فِي عِبَادِكَ ٱلصَّلِحِينَ ٱلصَّلِحِينَ

Rabbi ʾawziʿnī ʾan ʾaškura niʿmataka llatī ʾanʿamta ʿalayya wa-ʿalā wālidayya wa-ʾan ʾaʿmala ṣāliḥan tarḍāhu wa-ʾadḫilnī bi-raḥmatika fī ʿibādika ṣ-ṣāliḥīna.

Source: Sura 27:19 (An-Naml)

My Lord, grant me to be grateful for the grace You have granted me and my parents, and (grant me to) do good that is pleasing to You, and accept me in Your mercy among Your righteous servants.

260

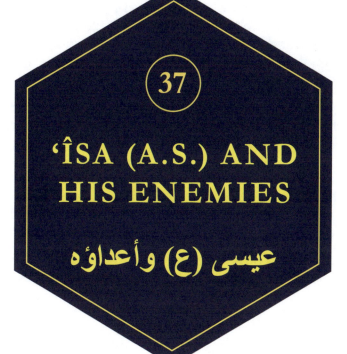

37

'ÎSA (A.S.) AND HIS ENEMIES

عيسى (ع) وأعداؤه

'Îsa (a.s.) and His Enemies

The scholars were very unhappy with 'Îsa (a.s.) because he taught things that were strange and new to them. They began to spread lies about him. They claimed that he was a magician and used tricks to deceive people. They added that he was an impostor pretending to be a messenger of God. And yes, you heard right, they even accused him of insulting the emperor and inciting a popular uprising!

So, what did they do with all these false accusations? They went to the emperor and the Roman authorities and presented their accusations. They hoped that the emperor would arrest and punish 'Îsa (a.s.) so that they could retain their power and influence. One of the scholars, a man with a stern look and a loud voice, came before the emperor and said, "Your Majesty, this man named 'Îsa (a.s.) is a danger to us all! Not only is he insulting your rule, but he is also calling the people to revolt!"

The king gave the order to arrest 'Îsa (a.s.) because these were offenses punishable by death. So, he sent out his soldiers to find him. A spy told the soldiers where 'Îsa (a.s.) was hiding with his twelve disciples.

When 'Îsa (a.s.) heard the clanking of the approaching soldiers' armor, he knew that they had come to arrest him. However, he remained calm and said to his disciples, "Do not be afraid. Trust in Allah (s.w.t.) and remain steadfast in faith."

What happened after the arrest of 'Îsa (a.s.) is reported differently.

Some believe that Allah (s.w.t.) answered his prayer immediately and miraculously got him out of the house before the soldiers could seize him. The spy, who looked very much like 'Îsa (a.s.), was instead arrested by the soldiers and thrown into prison. According to this version, 'Îsa (a.s.) will surely be raised to heaven by Allah (s.w.t.). However, the spy, whom everyone thought was 'Îsa, was crucified the following day. 'Îsa's (a.s.) disciples and his followers were saddened and horrified by the execution, but they always remembered what 'Îsa (a.s.) had preached and the miracles he had performed.

In another version, it is narrated that Allah (s.w.t.) raised 'Îsa (a.s.) directly to heaven when the soldiers came to arrest him.

Christians, on the other hand, believe that it was indeed 'Îsa (a.s.) whom they had arrested and crucified. And that 'Îsa (a.s.) rose again after three days and ascended to heaven. This is why Christians still celebrate Easter today.

One of the important lessons from this story is that it is crucial to trust Allah (s.w.t.) in all situations. 'Îsa (a.s.) helped this through dangerous times. We also see the value of honesty and justice and how important it is to always stick to the truth and act fairly. Lies only lead to more problems.

Sources: The Holy Qur'an:

Sura 3, verses 45-60 | Sura 4, verses 157-158 | Sura 5, verses 110-120 | Sura 23, verse 50.

HADITH

قال ابن عباس: لما أراد الله إن يرفع عيسى إليه خرج إلى أصحابه وهم اثنا
عشر رجلا، وهم الحواريون أصحاب عيسى المقربين، ثم قال: أيكم يلقى عليه
شبهي فيقتل مكاني ويكون معي في درجتي؟ فقام شاب من أحدثهم سنا ـ وهكذا
الشباب دائما إذا اقتنعوا بالدين والإيمان وتلبسوا به مستعدون بالتضحية في
سبيل الله ـ فقام أحدثهم سنا فقال: أنا، فقال عيسى: اجلس، فلما أعاد عليهم،
فقال الشاب: أنا، فقال: نعم أنت ذاك، فألقي عليه شبه عيسى على هذا الشاب،
ورفع عيسى، يعني الأصلي من روزنة كانت في البيت، يعني فتحة رفعه
الله إليه إلى السماء، قال: وجاء الطلب من اليهود، أصحاب المؤامرة الذين
يريدون القبض على عيسى وقتله، فاخذوا الشبيه فقتلوه، ثم صلبوه

Ibn Abbas said: "When Allah decided to raise Îsa to Himself, Îsa went out to his companions, who were twelve men, the followers of Îsa, his closest confidants. Then he said, 'Who among you will be like me and be killed in my place and be with me in my rank?' A young man among them, the youngest - as is often the case with young people when they are convinced of faith and accept it, ready to sacrifice in the way of Allah - stood up. Îsa said, 'Sit down.' When he repeated his question, the young man said again, 'I will.' Îsa said, 'Yes, you are.' Thus, the similitude of Îsa was cast upon that young man, and Îsa, the original, was lifted to the sky by Allah from an opening in the house which signified a window. Then the Jews, the conspirators who wanted to capture and kill Îsa, came and took the young man who looked like Îsa and killed him, then crucified him."

Abu Shu'bah in his Musannaf (31876), and his chain of traditions is
considered authentic according to the conditions laid down by Imam Muslim

DUA

PRAYER FOR BENEVOLENCE AND UNITY AMONG ALL BELIEVERS

رَبَّنَا ٱغْفِرْ لَنَا وَلِإِخْوَٰنِنَا ٱلَّذِينَ سَبَقُونَا بِٱلْإِيمَٰنِ وَلَا تَجْعَلْ فِي قُلُوبِنَا غِلًّا
لِّلَّذِينَ ءَامَنُوا۟ رَبَّنَآ إِنَّكَ رَءُوفٌ رَّحِيمٌ

Rabbanā ġfir lanā wa-li-'iḫwāninā lladīna sabaqūnā bi-l-'īmāni wa-lā taġ'al fī qulūbinā ġillan li-lladīna 'āmanū rabbanā 'innaka ra'ūfun raḥīmunī.

Source: Sura 59:10 (al-ḥašr)

Our Lord, forgive us and our brothers who have gone before us in faith and do not let resentment against the believers enter our hearts. Our Lord! You are truly kind and merciful.

38

GOD'S MESSENGERS TO OTHER PEOPLES

أنبياء الله إلى الشعوب الأخرى

GOD'S MESSENGERS TO OTHER PEOPLES

You already know many messengers that Allah (s.w.t.) sent to all the world to spread his message.

Take, for example, the Prophet Hûd (a.s.). He was sent to the people of 'Ad. These were extremely strong people, but unfortunately, they did not always use their strength for good. Hûd (a.s.) taught them that they should use their strength wisely and be just.

Then there was the Prophet Sâlih (a.s.). He was sent to the people of Thamûd who were famous for their ability to build beautiful houses in the mountains. Sâlih (a.s.) told them that they should be grateful for the gifts that Allah (s.w.t.) had granted them and that they should honor Him.

Not forgetting Lût (a.s.) who was sent to a people who had bad habits. Lût (a.s.) tried to show them the importance of living morally and treating each other with respect.

Shu'ayb (a.s.), another prophet, was sent to a people who loved to trade and often cheated. Shu'ayb (a.s.) taught them that honesty and fairness in trade are extremely important.

Then there was Dhul-Qarnayn (a.s.), who was a righteous king and traveled through many countries. He helped the people and taught them how to build their country and defend it against their enemies.

Not to be forgotten is 'Îsa (a.s.), whose story we have just heard.

These are by no means all the prophets of Allah (s.w.t.)! It is said that there were thousands of prophets that Allah (s.w.t.) sent at different times and to different regions of the world to help people find the right path. And there is one special message that all the prophets had in common and that is important! They all spread the core message that there is only one God, and that is Allah (s.w.t.). There is only Him who deserves our worship.

History teaches us that sincerity, gratitude, self-control, modesty, and the thirst for knowledge are important virtues that the Prophets of Allah (s.w.t.) spread and that should still be important to us today. Let us keep all these wonderful teachings in our hearts and do our best to be good people who are there for others and honor Allah (s.w.t.).

Sources: The Holy Qur'an:

Sura 2, verse 136 | Sura 4, verses 163-165 | Sura 6, verses 84-90 | Sura 42, verse 13.

HADITH

قال ابن كثير: أي وما من أمة خلت من بني آدم، إلا وقد بعث الله تعالى إليهم النذر

تفسير ابن كثير

Ibn Kathir said: "And there is no community among the sons of Adam to which Allah has not sent a warner."

Tafsir Ibn Katir

DUA

PRAYER FOR GUIDANCE TO THE RIGHT PATH

اللَّهُمَّ اهْدِنِي وَسَدِّدْنِي وَاذْكُرْ بِالْهُدَى هِدَايَتَكَ الطَّرِيقَ

Allahuma ahdini wasadidni wadhkur bialhudaa hidayataka tariqa.

O Allah, guide me, make me steadfast, and remember with guidance the path You lead.

Source: Sahih Muslim 2725a

THE STORY OF
THE ELEPHANT
ARMY

39

قصة أصحاب الفيل

THE STORY OF THE ELEPHANT ARMY

In a distant land called Yemen, there lived a king called Abraha. King Abraha was powerful and had a huge army, but there was something that bothered him a lot.

People still traveled from far away to Mecca to visit the Ka'ba, which Ibrâhîm (a.s.) and Isma'il (a.s.) had once built. Although the people living here worshipped idols, many people still came to the Ka'ba. There they traded in goods from all over the world and were entertained by the Arab tribe of Quraish.

But Abraha wanted people to come to a large temple he had built in his capital instead. He wanted to show everyone that he was the most powerful king. However, the people continued their pilgrimage to Mecca and visited the Ka'ba instead of traveling to Yemen.

One day, King Abraha was furious and said to his ministers, "I will go to Mecca with my army and destroy the Ka'ba! Then all the people will come to my temple and pray here!" What King Abraha did not know was that the Ka'ba was and still is a very, very sacred place and that Allah (s.w.t.) watches over the Ka'ba. King Abraha had a special army, and guess what made it so special? Huge elephants that Abraha had brought from India! So, he decided to have these mighty elephants, ridden by big and strong soldiers, attack Mecca.

The people of Mecca heard about Abraha's plan and were worried. They did not know how they could stop the army with the huge elephants. They were already thinking of surrendering, but one of the leaders in Mecca, Abdul Muttalib, said to the people, "Let us pray and ask Allah (s.w.t.) for protection. Only He can save us and the Ka'ba."

And then, as the elephant army approached the Ka'ba, something miraculous happened. The largest elephant suddenly refused to move! It simply sat down and did not move, no matter how hard the soldiers pushed it. Suddenly, a flock of small birds appeared in the sky, each carrying small stones in their claws. The birds rained the pebbles down on King Abraha's army. The elephants panicked, ran around wildly and the attack on Mecca and the Ka'ba failed. The entire army retreated to Yemen in defeat. There, King Abraha raged at the defeat.

What can we learn from this story? We learn that it is important to be respectful and humble and not to try to harm others. Even a powerful king with a large army can do nothing against the power of Allah (s.w.t.).

> **Sources:** The Holy Qur'an:
>
> Sura 105, verses 1-5.

HADITH

ثَبَتَ عَنِ المِسْوَرِ بْنِ مَخْرَمَةَ -رَضِيَ الله عنه- في حديثه الطويل لصلح الحديبية، قال: وسَارَ النَّبِيُّ -صَلَّى اللهُ عليه وسلَّمَ- حتَّى إذَا كانَ بالثَّنِيَّةِ الَّتِي يُهْبَطُ عليهم منها بَرَكَتْ به رَاحِلَتُهُ، فقالَ النَّاسُ: حَلْ حَلْ، فألَحَّتْ، فقالوا: خَلأَتِ القَصْوَاءُ، خَلأَتِ القَصْوَاءُ، فقالَ النَّبِيُّ -صَلَّى اللهُ عليه وسلَّمَ-: ما خَلأَتِ القَصْوَاءُ، وما ذاكَ لَها بخُلُقٍ، ولَكِنْ حَبَسَهَا حَابِسُ الفِيلِ

It is reported from Al-Musawwir ibn Makhrama (r.a.) in his detailed account of the Treaty of Hudaybiya that he said: "The Prophet, blessings, and peace of Allah be upon him, continued on his way until he reached Thaniyya, the place where his mount stopped. The people said, 'This is a rest, this is a rest' and insisted. They said, 'The Quraysh have canceled the terms (of the treaty)!' The Prophet (blessings and peace of Allah be upon him) replied: 'It is not a break, nor is there anything wrong with it. But it is Allah who has blocked it, just as He blocked the elephants.'"

Narrated by Al-Bukhari

DUA

PRAYER FOR FORGIVENESS OF MISDEEDS AND SINS

رَّبَّنَا إِنَّنَا سَمِعْنَا مُنَادِيًا يُنَادِي لِلْإِيمَٰنِ أَنْ ءَامِنُوا۟ بِرَبِّكُمْ فَـَٔامَنَّا رَبَّنَا فَٱغْفِرْ لَنَا ذُنُوبَنَا وَكَفِّرْ عَنَّا سَيِّـَٔاتِنَا وَتَوَفَّنَا مَعَ ٱلْأَبْرَارِ، رَبَّنَا وَءَاتِنَا مَا وَعَدتَّنَا عَلَىٰ رُسُلِكَ وَلَا تُخْزِنَا يَوْمَ ٱلْقِيَٰمَةِ إِنَّكَ لَا تُخْلِفُ ٱلْمِيعَادَ

Rabbanā 'innanā sami'nā munādiyan yunādī li-l-'īmāni 'an 'āminū bi-rabbikum fa-'āmannā rabbanā fa-ġfir lanā ḍunūbanā wa-kaffir 'annā sayyi'ātinā wa-tawaffanā ma'a l-'abrāri. rabbanā wa-'ātinā mā wa'adtanā 'alā rusulika wa-lā tuḫzinā yawma l-qiyāmati 'innaka lā tuḫlifu l-mī'āda.

Source: Sura 3:193-194 ('ā l'imrā n)

Our Lord, verily we heard a preacher calling to faith (and saying), "Believe in your Lord!" and so we believe. Our Lord, therefore, forgive us our sins and blot out our iniquities, and let us merge with the pious. Our Lord and grant us what You have promised us through Your messengers, and do not lead us into disgrace on the Day of Resurrection. Indeed, You do not break (Your) promise.

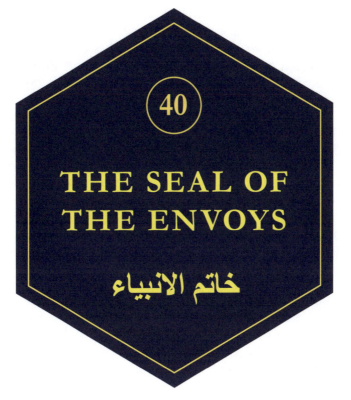

40

THE SEAL OF THE ENVOYS

خاتم الانبياء

THE SEAL OF THE ENVOYS

ver 1400 years ago, a young boy was born into a wealthy family in Mecca. His name was Muhammad (s.a.w.), son of Abdullah and Amina. However, Abdullah died before his son was born, so his name was given to him by his grandfather Abdul Muttalib, a respected man in Mecca. Amina and Abdul Muttalib both had strange dreams in which they saw that Muhammad (s.a.w.) was to become a special man.

Back then, it was common for children from noble families to spend some time with Bedouins in the desert. It was believed that life in the desert made them stronger and helped them to grow up naturally and healthy. Muhammad (s.a.w.) was also given to a dear woman named Halima, who became his foster mother. Halima was poor and lived with her family as a Bedouin in the desert. Imagine how Muhammad (s.a.w.) saw the vast desert around him as a young boy. He played in the sand, watched the camels, and learned how to survive in the desert.

Halima said that there had been many blessings since Muhammad (s.a.w.) had been with them. The camels gave more milk, and the harvest was richer than ever before. She knew that there was something incredibly special in this little boy. When Muhammad (s.a.w.) was four years old, he returned to his family in Mecca. Although it was difficult for Halima to say goodbye to him, she was glad that she had been able to accompany him on part of his journey.

Muhammad's (s.a.w.) mother Amina decided to take her son to his father's grave. They made their way to Yathrib, where Abdullah was buried. Muhammad (s.a.w.) was still young and he could not understand what a grave was, but he felt his mother's love and saw how important this place was to her. On the way back, however, something sad and terrible happened, Muhammad's (s.a.w.) mother Amina suddenly fell ill and passed away.

Little Muhammad (s.a.w.) was only six years old and now had to say goodbye to his beloved mother; but he was not completely alone. His grandfather Abdul Muttalib took him in and looked after him lovingly. Abdul Muttalib was still an important figure in Mecca and often took the young Muhammad (s.a.w.) to meetings with the elders of the city. Muhammad (s.a.w.) would sometimes sit quietly and listen to the conversations. He learned a lot, and everyone who saw him felt that he had a special wisdom.

Sadly, the next tragedy happened. When Muhammad was just eight years old, his beloved grandfather Abdul Muttalib (r.a.) passed away. It was a difficult time for him.

Muhammad ended up living with his uncle Abu Tâlib. He was a good man, but he did not have many possessions. This did not bother Muhammad because he was modest, hardworking, and helpful. As a young boy, Muhammad (s.a.w.) helped herd the sheep and goats. He would get up early and take the animals into the mountains to look for fresh grass. Living in nature made him strong and gave him plenty of time to think.

When Muhammad (s.a.w.) grew a little older, he also accompanied his uncle on trading trips. They traveled to distant lands and traded with many different people. One day, Muhammad sold one of his camels in Mecca, but then he noticed that the camel was lame. He went to the man and spoke to him about it. The man was astonished when Muhammad (s.a.w.) offered to take the camel back and refund the purchase price. This was extremely unusual in Mecca at the time and showed how sincere and just Muhammad (s.a.w.) was. He did not want anyone to be treated unfairly or to feel that they had been cheated. People found out about this and called him Al-Amin, which means "the trustworthy one". People often asked him for advice because they knew that he was both wise and just.

One day it rained so heavily in Mecca that the streets were flooded. The Ka'ba and many other buildings were severely damaged because the rain washed out the foundations. The people of Mecca were worried and sad because the Ka'ba was important to them. They decided to act quickly and rebuild the shrine. Everyone helped, Men, women, and even children brought stones and other building materials.

After a few days of hard work, the Ka'ba was almost rebuilt. Then it was time to put the sacred black stone back in its place in the Ka'ba. And that is when a big fight broke out between the different tribes of Mecca! Each tribe wanted the honor of putting the black stone in its place and to be remembered for it forever. The dispute became increasingly heated, and some people even thought it might come to a fight. Then a wise old man got the crowd's attention with a good idea. He suggested that the first man to come to the Ka'ba the next morning should decide who would be allowed to put the Black Stone in its place. Everyone agreed.

The next morning, the people came to the Ka'ba early, eager to see who would be the first. And who was the first to come to the Ka'ba that morning? It was the young Muhammad (s.a.w.). The people were very relieved and exclaimed, "This is the trustworthy one! We are pleased with him as a mediator!"

Muhammad (s.a.w.) listened to the problem and then came up with a wonderful solution. He laid a large cloth on the ground and placed the Black Stone in the center. Then he asked a representative of each tribe to hold a part of the cloth. Together they lifted the cloth and brought the stone close to the designated place in the Ka'ba. Muhammad (s.a.w.) himself then carefully placed the stone with his own hands. In this way, Muhammad (s.a.w.) prevented further disputes and showed how important it is to work together and find peaceful solutions.

However, although the Ka'ba was rebuilt, many people in Mecca continued to worship idols. They had erected small statues and thought that these would bring them luck. They thought more of themselves, their families, and their tribes than of others. Life in Mecca was hard, and many people were extremely poor, but the rich people did not help them. People were selfish and did not even think of doing good deeds. Many of them did not believe that one day they would be accountable to Allah (s.w.t.) and therefore they did not care about the welfare of their fellow human beings.

But the young Muhammad (s.a.w.) was different. He always thought of the poor and helped where he could. He knew that it was important to take care of his fellow human beings and to have a good heart.

One day, Muhammad (s.a.w.) received an interesting offer. A wealthy woman named Khadija was looking for someone who could help her run her trading business. Khadija was a very clever and respected woman in Mecca. She was a widow; her husband had died. Many men wanted to marry her, but she turned them all down. Khadija had heard about Muhammad's (s.a.w.) honesty and reliability and thought that he was just the right person to help her. So, she hired Muhammad (s.a.w.) and sent him on a trading trip with a slave named Maysarah. During the journey, Muhammad (s.a.w.) worked hard and proved his skills as a merchant. Maysarah observed him and was impressed by his character and behavior.

After their return, Muhammad (s.a.w.) and Maysarah told Khadija everything that had happened and brought back a lot of money that they had earned through fair trade.

Khadija was so impressed by his skills and character that she wanted to marry Muhammad (s.a.w.). And do you know what? Muhammad (s.a.w.) felt the same way! So, they got married and started a family. Khadija supported Muhammad (s.a.w.) in everything he did, and they had children together. Their marriage was an example of love, respect, and partnership. Muhammad (s.a.w.) continued his efforts to help the people around him and to tell them about Allah (s.w.t.).

However, Muhammad (s.a.w.) felt a great inner restlessness and the need to reflect on life and its meaning. He therefore often withdrew to the cave of Hira, located in a mountain near Mecca. There he thought about creation and people.

One day, when Muhammad (s.a.w.) was meditating in the cave, the angel Jibril appeared to him. Jibril brought him a book from

Allah (s.w.t.), a part of the Holy Qur'an. He called out with a strong voice, "Read!"

Muhammad (s.a.w.) looked at the angel, looked at the book and his heart pounded with excitement. "I can't read," he replied quietly. But the angel repeated emphatically, "Read!" Muhammad (s.a.w.) was confused and said again, "I really don't know how to read."

Then the angel embraced him tightly and said in a gentle voice, "Read in the name of your Lord who created. He created man from a small germ. Recite! Your Lord is the Most Generous, Who teaches man through writing. He has taught man things that he did not know before."

These were the first words of the Holy Qur'an that Allah (s.w.t.) revealed to Muhammad (s.a.w.) through the angel Jibrīl. Muhammad (s.a.w.) was astonished and felt that this was an important message. He ran home to his wife Khadija and told her everything.

Khadija took Muhammad (s.a.w.) to Waraqah ibn Nawfal, who was a scholar and relative of hers. They told him about what Muhammad (s.a.w.) had experienced in Mount Hira. He described exactly how the angel Jibril had come to him and delivered the words of Allah (s.w.t.) to him. Waraqah listened attentively and his eyes widened in amazement. Then he said in a firm voice, "Oh, this is wonderful! What you have experienced, Muhammad (s.a.w.), is what happened to the Prophet Musa. You are a messenger of Allah (s.w.t.) who was chosen to bring His words to the people."

Muhammad (s.a.w.) was surprised and moved by Waraqah's words. He now understood that Allah (s.w.t.) had assigned him a great task and that he would be the last among the prophets. One day, when Muhammad (s.a.w.) and Khadija were praying together, Ali (r.a.), the son of Abu Tâlib, came to them. He was still a boy, but very curious. He asked, "What are you doing?"

Muhammad (s.a.w.) smiled and replied, "We pray to Allah (s.w.t.) and thank Him." Then he told Ali (r.a.) about the Qur'an and the beautiful words that the angel Jibrīl had given him. He also explained to Ali (r.a.) what constitutes a Muslim - namely to believe in one God, Allah (s.w.t.), to do good deeds, and to care for the people around him. This was the first time that someone explained what it meant to be a Muslim.

Ali's (a.s.) eyes lit up with excitement. "I want to be a Muslim too!" he exclaimed. Muhammad (s.a.w.) was happy about this and took Ali (r.a.) in his arms. From that day on, Ali (r.a.) was among the first Muslims. Some of Muhammad's (s.a.w.) friends also joined, and so the community of Muslims began to grow. Many of the poor and even slaves joined.

Allah (s.w.t.) began to reveal the Qur'an to Muhammad (s.a.w.) bit by bit. Yes, that is right - the Qur'an did not just come suddenly, but over many years, in bits and pieces! Muhammad (s.a.w.) tried to explain the words of Allah (s.w.t.) to the rich and powerful people of Mecca. He said to them, "Please, listen to your hearts and act justly! Allah (s.w.t.) wants you to be good to each other, help the poor and not cheat!"

But the rich people just laughed and said, "Why should we listen to you, Muhammad (s.a.w.)? We have enough money and power. We do not need any change!" They just wanted to carry on as before and did not care about the poor or about acting justly.

Muhammad (s.a.w.) was sad about this. He wanted people to lead a better life. And then Allah (s.w.t.) spoke to him again, "Go out and call the people to me loud and clear! Tell them about justice, sharing, and the good life they can lead if they listen to Me!"

Muhammad (s.a.w.) felt encouraged by Allah's (s.w.t.) words. He climbed a hill close to the Ka'ba and called the people together. He asked the gathered crowd, "What would you say if I told you that there is a great army waiting behind this mountain, ready to attack us? Would you believe me?"

The people replied, "Yes, of course we would believe you! You are known to be trustworthy and honest." Thereupon Muhammad (s.a.w.) said, "Then believe me when I tell you that I am a Messenger of Allah (s.w.t.) and He has given me a message for all of you. You must stop paying homage to false gods and pray only to Allah (s.w.t.). We must be just, take care of the poor, and lead a good life. If you do not stop worshipping false gods, Allah (s.w.t.) will be displeased with you. And then I will not be able to help even my best friends and relatives."

Through this example, Muhammad (s.a.w.) wanted to show people that it is just as important to listen to the spiritual warning he gave them as it is to listen to a warning of a threat from a foreign army.

However, the people of Mecca reacted differently to Muhammad's (s.a.w.) warnings and advice. Some were curious and wanted to know more about how they could honor Allah (s.w.t.) and lead a better life. These people began to listen to Muhammad (s.a.w.) and consider themselves Muslims, but there were also many, especially the rich and powerful, who were angry at what Muhammad (s.a.w.) said. They were angry that he was threatening their traditions and questioning their power.

"What is this, Muhammad (s.a.w.)?" one of the rich men exclaimed. "We have always worshipped our idols, and now you say we should give that up. Why should we pay attention to you?"

The rich began to plot to silence Muhammad (s.a.w.). They made up lies about him and mocked him in front of others. Some even tried to threaten and harm him and his followers. Muhammad (s.a.w.), however, remained steadfast. He was not afraid of the rich because he knew that he was spreading the important message of Allah (s.w.t.). He felt that it was his duty to help the people of Mecca and beyond to find the right path.

But many rich people were still stubborn. They did not want to give up what they had, and they did not want to share. They even began to treat Muhammad (s.a.w.) and those who followed him badly.

Muhammad's (s.a.w.) dear uncle Abu Tâlib was very worried about his nephew and asked him to be careful. "Muhammad (s.a.w.), my nephew," he said, "I am very worried about you. The rich are not happy about what you say, and I fear they may harm you." But Muhammad (s.a.w.) did not care.

Even when tempted by the rich to make Muhammad (s.a.w.) a wealthy man, even a king, he boldly replied, "Even if you were to put the sun in my right hand and the moon in my left hand to make me stop, I would not stop until Allah's (s.w.t.) message is spread or I give my life for it."

The rich people were incredibly angry. "If that's the case, we'll expel you Muslims!" they shouted. And they did. They did not allow the Muslims to buy food, and no one was allowed to trade with them.

They also decided to expel the Muslims from Mecca and recorded this in a treaty. Muhammad (s.a.w.) and the other Muslims were driven out of the city and banished to a dry ravine. It was an extremely hard life there, without enough water and food.

The treaty that the rich people of Mecca had written to banish the Muslims had been kept in the Ka'ba. One day, however, the people discovered that termites had almost completely eaten away the treaty, except for the words "In the name of your Lord" - that was all that was left. The people of Mecca saw this as a sign and believed that it was God's will to lift the banishment of the Muslims. So, after three hard years, the Muslims were finally allowed to return to the city of Mecca.

But imagine that although they were allowed to return, they were still not left in peace. The rich people of Mecca still did not want the Muslims to practice their faith freely. A short time later, Abu Tâlib and Khadija died.

The idolaters therefore thought that Muhammad (s.a.w.) was weakened and a man named Abu Jahl tried to strangle him while he was praying in the Ka'ba. However, other Muslims helped Muhammad (s.a.w.) and beat Abu Jahl back.

Then, one night, while Muhammad (s.a.w.) was sleeping in Mecca, a special mount called Buraq came to him. Imagine, Buraq was a heavenly creature that was bigger than a donkey but smaller than a horse and could fly incredibly fast! Jibrīl, the angel, said to Muhammad (s.a.w.), "Mount up, we have a special journey ahead of us!" And they flew together through the night.

First, they flew to Jerusalem, the holy city that had also been of immense importance to other prophets. Once there, Muhammad (s.a.w.) prayed together with the earlier prophets on a mountain. Today, the Al-Aqsa Mosque stands on this very spot.

Allah (s.w.t.) showed Muhammad (s.a.w.) the heavens and sent him important messages and wisdom to share with the Muslims, including the importance of daily prayer.

When Muhammad (s.a.w.) returned to Mecca, only a few moments had passed, although it had felt like a long journey. He told people about his experiences, but many idolaters did not want to believe him. They thought it would be impossible to travel so far in a single night. They planned to assassinate Muhammad (s.a.w.).

When Muhammad (s.a.w.) and his friend Abu Bakr (r.a.) heard about this in Mecca, they left the city and made their way to Yathrib, which is now called Medina. They knew that they were in constant danger because the idolaters were hot on their heels and wanted to kill them. They decided to hide in a cave called Thaur, located in a mountain near Mecca. They sat there in the darkness of the cave and waited while they were searched for. The brave Abu Bakr (r.a.) was very worried about Muhammad (s.a.w.). He said, "O Prophet if one of them looks closely, he will see us!" Muhammad (s.a.w.), who was always full of trust in Allah (s.w.t.), reassured him and said, "Do not be afraid, for Allah (s.w.t.) is with us."

Then something amazing happened! Allah (s.w.t.) sent a spider that wove a large web over the entrance of the cave with lightning speed, and a dove laid its eggs near the entrance.

When the idolaters arrived at the cave and saw the spider's web and the dove's eggs, they thought that no one could be in the cave, otherwise the web and the eggs would be destroyed. So, Allah (s.w.t.) protected Muhammad (s.a.w.) and Abu Bakr (r.a.). The other Muslims who remained in Mecca were also miraculously protected by Him.

Muhammad (s.a.w.) and Abu Bakr (r.a.) finally made their way to Yathrib, where many Muslims were already living and had invited them there. This journey became known as the Hijrah. In Medina, Muhammad (s.a.w.) and his companion were warmly welcomed. Many other Muslims flocked from Mecca to Yathrib to seek refuge from the idolaters, but even there they were not completely safe. The idolaters from Mecca still wanted to fight against them. There were several battles.

The first major battle was the Battle of Badr. The Muslims had only a small army compared to the idolaters. Muhammad (s.a.w.) said to his warriors, "Be brave and steadfast, and trust that Allah (s.w.t.) will help us!"

And indeed, despite their numerical inferiority, the Muslims defeated the idolaters with Allah's (s.w.t.) help. That was truly amazing!

Then there was another battle, known as the Battle of Uhud. The Muslims were initially successful, but then something unexpected happened, some of them left their posts too early, thinking that victory was certain. The idolaters seized this opportunity and attacked again. The Muslims suffered heavy losses and the Prophet Muhammad (s.a.w.) was also injured. However, they prevailed despite the superiority of the enemy army. After the battle, Muhammad (s.a.w.) said to the Muslims, "We must learn from our mistakes and always be disciplined and obedient."

The battles continued, including the Battle of Khandaq, in which the Muslims dug a deep pit around Medina to protect the city. The idolaters could not get over it. After a terrible storm with heavy rain fell upon them, they were finally forced to retreat.

Eventually, a peace treaty was signed between the Muslims and the Meccans, the Treaty of Hudaybiyyah. A few years later, the Muslims were finally able to enter Mecca without bloodshed, and the Prophet Muhammad (s.a.w.) generously forgave all those who had previously harmed him and the Muslims. He invited people to embrace Islam and they professed to be Muslims. They stopped worshipping idols and only worshipped Allah (s.w.t.) in the Ka'ba. And finally, people listened to Him!

During a sermon on his last journey to Mecca, Muhammad (s.a.w.) said to the assembled people, "Hear my words well, for I know not whether I shall ever be among you again after this year. Your blood, your property, and your honor are sacred to each other, as this day in this month is sacred in this city."

He emphasized the uniqueness of Allah (s.w.t.) and said, "Be certain that there is no god but Allah (s.w.t.)." Muhammad (s.a.w.) added, "You are all descended from Adam (s.a.w.), and Adam (s.a.w.) was created from earth. There is no precedence of an Arab over a non-Arab, and of a non-Arab over an Arab, nor a white over a black, and a black over a white, except in righteousness."

He also exhorted people to adhere to the teachings of Islam, to live in justice and brotherhood, and to respect the rights of women. He also called on them to carry the message of Allah (s.w.t.) after his death. He said to the crowd, "I have left you two precious treasures, the Qur'an and my example. Hold fast to them and you will surely walk on the right path."

After the Messenger of Allah (s.w.t.) uttered these words, a very last message of the Qur'an was sent down from heaven, "Today I have perfected your faith and poured out My mercy on you, and I have chosen Islam as the path you should follow in life."

The story of Muhammad (s.a.w.) teaches us many valuable lessons, such as steadfastness in faith. Muhammad (s.a.w.) remained steadfast in his faith and mission despite all opposition and difficulties. Moreover, Muhammad (s.a.w.) shows us the importance of kindness and forgiveness. Even when he had the opportunity to take revenge on those who had tried to harm him, he chose the path of forgiveness. Equality and justice are also central themes in Muhammad's (s.a.w.) life. He taught that all people are equal, regardless of their origin, race, or social status. This encourages us to treat all people with respect and dignity and to stand up for justice. Muhammad (s.a.w.) also placed great emphasis on education. He encouraged people to learn and share their knowledge with others. This emphasizes how important education and knowledge are for personal growth and the development of a community.

The story of Muhammad (s.a.w.), the Prophet, is a model for living a life of decency, faith, goodness, justice, and devotion.

Sources: The Holy Qur'an:

Sura 96, verses 1-5 | Sura 17, verse 1 | Sura 8, verses 41-19 | Sura 3, verses 121-180 | Sura 5, verse 3.

HADITH

فُضِّلْتُ على الأنبياءِ بِسِتٍّ: أُعطيتُ جوامعَ الكلِمِ ونُصِرْتُ بالرُّعبِ وأُحِلَّتْ لي الغنائمُ وجُعِلت لي الأرضُ طَهورًا ومسجدًا وأُرسِلْتُ إلى الخَلقِ كافَّةً وخُتِمَ بي النَّبِيُّونَ

[The Prophet (s.a.w.) said:] "I was favored over the prophets in six ways: I was given precise and complete ways of speech, I was granted victory by force, the spoils of war were allowed to me, the earth was designated as a place of purification and a place of prayer for me, I was sent to all mankind, and the prophets were sealed with my mission."

Sahih Ibn Hibban 2313

DUA

PRAISING ALLAH FOR HIS ALMIGHTY MAJESTY

ٱللَّهُ لَا إِلَٰهَ إِلَّا هُوَ ٱلْحَيُّ ٱلْقَيُّومُ لَا تَأْخُذُهُ سِنَةٌ وَلَا نَوْمٌ لَّهُ مَا فِي ٱلسَّمَٰوَٰتِ وَمَا فِي ٱلْأَرْضِ مَن ذَا ٱلَّذِي يَشْفَعُ عِندَهُ إِلَّا بِإِذْنِهِ يَعْلَمُ مَا بَيْنَ أَيْدِيهِمْ وَمَا خَلْفَهُمْ وَلَا يُحِيطُونَ بِشَيْءٍ مِّنْ عِلْمِهِ إِلَّا بِمَا شَاءَ وَسِعَ كُرْسِيُّهُ ٱلسَّمَٰوَٰتِ وَٱلْأَرْضَ وَلَا يَئُودُهُ حِفْظُهُمَا وَهُوَ ٱلْعَلِيُّ ٱلْعَظِيمُ

Allāhu lā 'ilāha 'illā huwa l-ḥayyu l-qayyūmu lā ta'ḥuḏuhū sina-tun wa-lā nawmun lahū mā fī s-samāwāti wa-mā fī l-'arḍi man ḏā llaḏī yašfaʿu ʿindahū 'illā bi-'iḏnihī yaʿlamu mā bayna 'aydīhim wa-mā ḫalfahum wa-lā yuḥīṭūna bi-šay'in min ʿilmihī 'illā bi-mā šā'a wasiʿa kursiyyuhu s-s-samāwāti wa-l-'arḍa wa-lā ya'ūduhū ḥifẓuhumā wa-huwa l-ʿaliyyu l-ʿaẓīmu.

Source: Sura 2:255 (al-ba-qara, "throne verse")

Allah, there is no god but Him, the Living, the Eternal. He is not seized by slumber or sleep. To Him belongs what is in the heavens and what is on earth. Who is there who could intercede with Him except with His permission? He knows what is before them and what is behind them, but they understand nothing of His knowledge except what He wills. Far does His throne extend over the heavens and the earth, and it is not difficult for Him to preserve them (both). And He is the High, the Exalted.

OTHER BOOKS BY ISLAM WAY AND IBRAHIM AL-ABADI

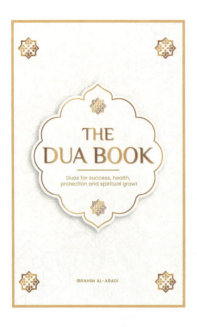

The Dua book

More than 260 duas with the original Arabic text, English translation, qr codes and audios of each supplication.

Available here:

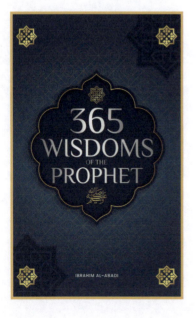

365 Wisdoms of the Prophet Muhammad

365 selected hadiths of the Prophet Muhammad.

Available here:

Dear reader,

Did you like this book? We welcome your suggestions for improvement, criticism and questions about the book.

The opinion and satisfaction of our readers is very important to us.

Therefore, please do not hesitate to contact us by sending an e-mail to **info@islamway-books.com**.

Yours sincerely

Ibrahim Al-Abadi and Islam Way

Printed in France by Amazon
Brétigny-sur-Orge, FR

19292289R10170